Manchester
cycle
Rides

Neil Simpson has asserted his rights to be
identified as the author of this work.

© Neil Simpson 2004

All rights reserved. No part of this publication may be
reproduced, stored in a retrieval system or transmitted,
in any form or by any means, electronic, mechanical,
photocopying, recording or otherwise, without prior
permission in writing from the publisher.
Published and printed by: Haynes Publishing, Sparkford,
Yeovil, Somerset BA22 7JJ.

British Library Cataloguing-in-Publication Data:
A catalogue record for this book is available
from the British Library.

ISBN 1 84425 026 1

While every effort has been taken to ensure the
accuracy of the information given in this book,
no liability can be accepted by the author or the
publishers for any loss, damage or injury caused by
errors in, or omissions from, the information given.

CONTENTS

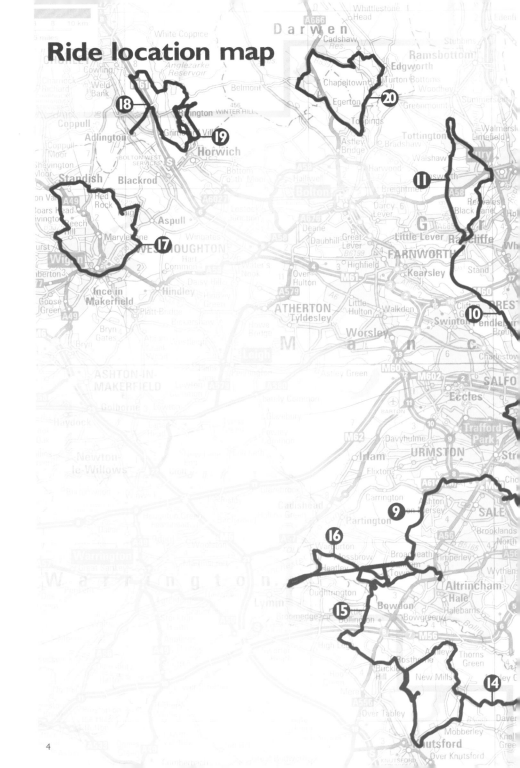

Ride location map

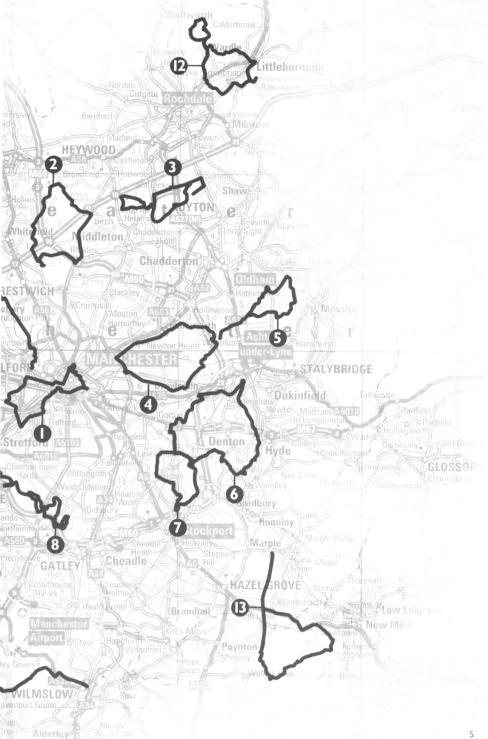

5

Foreword

Before I started work on these routes I thought I knew Manchester and its cycling reasonably well. After all, I had lived and worked here for many years. However, the experience of riding and researching these 20 routes came as a revelation. It is easy to forget, or perhaps to never know what diversity there is within the 10 boroughs of what we call Greater Manchester. Each has a character of its own and a unique combination of landscape and history. I hope this selection of routes in some way reflects that.

Exploring by bike is surely the best way to get to know the region. The relatively slow pace combined with the ability to cover so many kilometres gives a unique perspective, plus, of course it is healthy, harmless to the environment and much more fun than driving from place to place.

The routes are not designed as major physical challenges, nor are they for racing round. They are simply a selection of trails and roads that I think give a good introduction to the pleasures of exploring the region, and avoiding heavy or fast-moving traffic as far as practical or possible. Take them at a steady pace, appreciate the views and the attractions, and the many, many cups of tea it will take to get round them all. I hope you enjoy riding them as much as I have.

Neil Simpson

Introduction

Greater Manchester is the biggest conurbation in the northwest of England. Made up of 10 boroughs; Manchester, Trafford, Salford, Wigan, Bolton, Bury, Rochdale, Oldham, Tameside and Stockport, with a population of 2.5 million, this is an exciting region to explore. These rides are distributed across all 10 boroughs, and travelling by bike guarantees getting to know the area better than in any other way.

Manchester was the cradle of the industrial revolution in the 18th and 19th centuries. Many of the canals and railway lines that generated so much wealth and industry then have now become places for our recreation, and they feature in many of the routes in this book. Manchester is also a very modern place, a centre of technological development and sporting prowess. And most importantly for cyclists, it is surrounded by some of the finest cycling country to be found anywhere.

The 400km of cycle route featured here, 136km of which is car free, represents the best but really just a fraction of the possible rides that tease out what the area has to offer. From the industrial heritage of canals and mills, to the historic country houses and lanes of Cheshire, and the Pennine hills to the north and east, the variety of easily accessible terrain is unbeatable.

The selected routes are a pleasure to ride, pass interesting features or landmarks, and importantly, have places to stock up on tea and cake. The percentage of car-free riding varies from 0 to 90, but no route will put you on fast or dangerous roads or through long stretches of urban road, the only exception being the city centre circuit, which is best tackled on a Sunday, when traffic is lightest.

A word about the weather. By reputation Manchester is a rainy town. Well yes, of course, it does rain in Manchester, but not as much as you might think. The average rainfall is 809mm a year, less than Plymouth, Cardiff, Glasgow, Edinburgh and many other places in the UK, so don't be put off. On the other hand it's only sensible to be prepared, especially for rides that venture up into the hills where the weather turns very quickly. Modern waterproofs are light, easy to carry and a worthy investment, as newcomers can find getting cold and wet thoroughly miserable and off-putting.

MANCHESTER GENERAL CYCLING INFORMATION
A selection of bike shops

Bicycle Doctor, 68-70 Dickenson Rd,
  Rusholme, Manchester M14 5HF
  (tel 0161 224 1303)
Mike Cookson Cycles, 187-195 Bury New
  Road, Whitefield, Manchester M45 6GR
  (tel 0161 766 2633)
Bikehouse, 177 School Lane, Didsbury
  Manchester M19 1GN (tel 0161 443 1235)
Withington Cycles, 26 Burton Rd, Withington,
  Manchester M20 3EB (tel 0161 445 3492)
Ken Foster's Cycle Logic, 374 Barlow Moor
  Rd, Chorlton, Manchester M21 8AZ
  (tel 0161 881 7160)
Hirsts Cycles, 60-62 Chorley Rd, Manchester
  M27 5AD (tel 0161 794 2000)
Bardsleys Cycles, 482 Manchester Rd,
  Stockport SK4 5DL (tel 0161 432 4936)
Northwest Mountain Bike Centre, 249
  Stockport Rd, Cheadle SK8 2BS
  (tel 0161 428 3311)
Altrincham Bike Shack, 10 Oakfield Trading
  Estate, Oakfield Rd, Altrincham WA15 8EJ
  (tel 0161 929 9355)

The National Cycling Centre

Also known as the Manchester Velodrome,
this is Britain's best indoor cycle venue and has
proved one of world's finest and fastest tracks.
Home to our Olympic and Commonwealth
champions, the track also hosts regular local
racing and training sessions and offers
introductions to beginners in this most
exciting of cycling disciplines. If you would like
to hire a bike and give it a go contact the
Manchester Velodrome (tel 0161 223 2244, or
www.manchestervelodrome.com).

Cycling Projects

(formerly Cycling Project for the North
West) is a charity based in Salford which
promotes a number of very worthwhile
cycling initiatives including working with
young people in Manchester encouraging
them to ride bikes, improve their health and
learn useful new skills. The Wheels for All
project helps disabled people enjoy cycling
by providing adapted bikes for hire at selected
venues. To support these and other
worthwhile projects call tel 0161 745 9099
or go to www.cycling.org.uk.

The Greater Manchester Cycling Campaign

brings cyclists together from across Greater Manchester and represents their interests to local authorities and transport organisations. The campaign works for improved facilities and services for all cyclists and can be contacted at www.gmcc.org.uk, and email secretary@gmcc.org.uk. They can also put you in touch with more locally-based campaign groups.

The Fallowfield Loop Line or the Manchester Cycle Way

when complete, will be one of Britain's longest urban cycleways. Based upon the disused Fallowfield railway line the route is already an impressive car-free 'ring-road' around south and east Manchester. The path is wide and has a high-quality surface. Currently running from Chorlton round to Gorton and on, via the Ashton Canal, to Sport City (Ride 4) there are ambitious plans to extend the line into north Manchester and further west to join the Mersey Valley and Trans Pennine Trails. When those connections are in place there will be an exciting chance to link long car-free rides within urban Manchester.

Trans Pennine Trail

The Trans Pennine Trail or TPT is an important part of the National Cycle Network, an impressive coast-to-coast route linking Liverpool in the west to Hull in the east. The full journey is 344km (215 miles) of continuous trail, car free wherever possible. It is designed to be shared by walkers, cyclists and horse riders, usually on the same path, but occasionally on different 'strands' of the route. In Greater Manchester the TPT travels from Lymm (Ride 16), through the Mersey Valley (Rides 8 and 9), to Stockport (Ride 7) and the Tame Valley (Ride 8). Comprehensive route guides and up-to-date route information are found on www.transpenninetrail.org.uk.

Pennine Bridleway

This is another long-distance off-road trail conceived as a rider's (of horse and bike) alternative to the Pennine Way, although it will, of course, be open to walkers as well. The bridleway travels from the Peak District north along the Pennines to Northumberland. Not due for completion until 2008, the first part is now open. The Mary Townley Loop is an excellent circular 75km (47 mile) trail, the southern end of which passes just north of Rochdale and intersects with Ride 12. For more information see www.nationaltrails.co.uk.

Sustrans in Manchester

Sustrans is the national charity that works with local bodies to create the National Cycle Network (NCN), which by 2005 will be approaching 10,000 miles in length. The network is designed to serve local and national cycling. 30 per cent is traffic free, while the rest uses quiet lanes or calmed roads in urban areas.

The important routes in Greater Manchester are the east-west Trans Pennine Trail and the north-south Route Six, from Salford northwards (the Irwell Valley Trail route) continuing all the way to the Lake District. Sustrans has also taken the lead on the Fallowfield Loop Line, which will have useful local links. Many boroughs also have local routes forming useful links, and commuting or leisure routes which are part of the greater network. For more information see; www.sustrans.org.uk and www.sustransshop.co.uk.

BEST ROUTES FOR CHILDREN AND BEGINNERS

While it is difficult to prescribe routes as suitable or unsuitable for individual abilities, the following are best suited to accompanied children and beginners, as they are mostly car free, flat or both.

City Centre (1)
Tandle Hill to Hollins (3)
East Manchester Towpaths (4)
Reddish Vale and Loop Line (7)
Mersey Valley Riverside Trails (8)
Mersey Valley to Dunham Park (9)
Irwell Valley Trail (10)

St Peter's Square in the heart of the city.

Bury Circular (11)
Dunham Park to Tatton Park (15)
Altrincham to Lymm (16)
Lever Park Off-Road (19)

ROUTES TO COMBINE TO FORM LONGER RIDES

Once the Rides described have been completed you can link them together for more ambitious excursions. Just allow a little more time and go prepared for a longer day in the saddle. By then, you should be fit enough to cope easily.

- Rides 4 & 5 become a 29km (18 mile) figure-of-eight that starts close to the city centre on canal towpaths and goes all the way out to the edge of the Peak District.
- Rides 6 & 7 become a 31km (19 mile) loop that is nearly 60% car free.
- Rides 10 & 11 together add up to a 53km (33 mile) outing from the centre of Salford into the Pennine Hills.
- Rides 14 & 15 link Wilmslow with two major country estates across the Cheshire countryside, 54km (34 miles).
- Rides 9 and 16: the Altrincham to Lymm ride can be extended to include a visit to Dunham Park, or the Mersey Valley. The Dunham ride can be extended all the way to Lymm.

BIKES AND MANCHESTER PUBLIC TRANSPORT
Bikes on trains

The area is served by the largest network of train lines outside London, which makes it possible to get around relatively easily. The carriage of bikes is generally not a problem except at peak times when trains can be overcrowded. For information on trains and timetables see www.gmpte.gov.uk or tel 0161 228 7811. Textphone users should call tel 0870 241 2216.

Bikes on the Metro

Bikes aren't currently allowed on Manchester's Metrolink trams as the operator considers there to be insufficient space in the carriages. However the Metro is expanding and it is

THE OFF-ROAD CYCLING CODE

1 Stay on the trail
Only ride bridleways and byways
Avoid footpaths
Plan your route in advance
Use Explorer/Landranger maps

2 Tell someone where you are going
(and when you expect to be back)
If possible, leave a map of the ride at home

3 Give way to horses
Stop completely for horses – they can take fright and flight
If you do ride past, do it carefully after checking with the rider

4 Give way to walkers
Say 'hello' too!

5 Bunching is harassing
Ride in twos or threes

6 Prevent erosion
Don't skid deliberately

7 Close the gate behind you
(but if it is fastened open, leave it open)
Don't climb walls or force hedges

8 Stay mobile
Wear a helmet
A mobile phone can be a great aid
Carry a First Aid kit
Carry enough food and drink
Pack waterproofs and warm clothes

9 Take pride in your bike
Maintain it before you leave home
Carry essential spares and tools

10 Be tidy
Litter in the countryside is horrible
Guard against fire

11 Keep smiling

The Windmill at Haig on ride 17.

hoped that the new trams will be large enough to carry cycles, at least at off-peak times.

Bikes on Manchester towpaths

There is a total of 78km (49 miles) of canal in Greater Manchester, much of it open and ideal for cycling. However there is a restriction: it is necessary to have a permit (issued free) to ride the towpaths. You can request a permit online from www.britishwaterways.co.uk or by applying to British Waterways' regional office at Trafalgar House, Temple Court, Birchwood, Warrington WA3 6GD (tel 01925 847700).

By accepting the cycle permit, you are agreeing to follow the Waterways Code, and to cycle only on stretches classified as open to cyclists. Another excellent website is www.waterscape.com, which has complete and up-to-date details of which towpaths are accessible to cyclists and which are not, as well as plenty of interesting additional information on watery activities and events.

TOWPATH CYCLING CODE
- Give way to other people at all times.
- Warn others of your approach. Use a bell.
- Be polite. A 'hello' and 'thank you' mean a lot.
- Watch out for hazards. Slow down for pedestrians and bridges. Dismount if necessary.
- Ride at a gentle pace. Towpaths aren't for racing.
- Only use towpaths in daylight.
- Take care on wet and uneven surfaces.
- To cycle on towpaths you need a free permit.

TRAIL ETIQUETTE

Many of the off-road routes described here are in areas popular with walkers and horse riders. To ensure continued access and a pleasant day out it is important to ride responsibly and bear in mind the Off-road Cycling Code.

Surviving the traffic

Don't let heavy traffic put you off riding around a city. With assertiveness, awareness and a tad of fitness, you can claim your space on the tarmac and enjoy being in control of your journey.

There are bad and careless drivers and good cyclists. The reverse is also true. Safety depends on two factors: awareness of potential hazards and how to avoid them; and considerate cycling techniques designed to catch the attention of other drivers and help them to help you.

Cycling hazards

Left-hand bends

Indicate to request space as you swing round a left-hand bend so you don't get squeezed. Cars tend not to allow for your travel space. Indicate with your right arm.

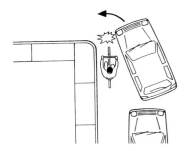

Drafting

Drafting or slipstreaming vehicles is fast, furious fun, so naturally, it is dangerous. Vehicles brake more quickly than bikes, especially in the wet.

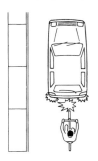

Gaps in your line of traffic

This can mean space is being left for a car outside your vision to turn into. Brake and approach with great care.

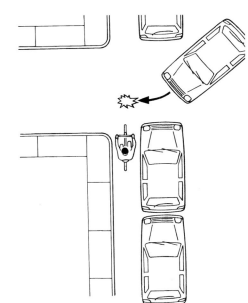

Bollards

These help pedestrians, but hinder cyclists. Anticipate that you may be squeezed, and request space by sticking out an arm in good time.

Car doors opening

Leave 1 metre between you and any parked cars. Catch the driver's eye in their wing mirror.

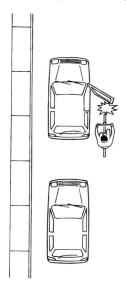

Being crushed by lorries or buses

Never get on the inside of buses, coaches or lorries going left. The most frequent cause of cycling fatalities is a rider being crushed as the vehicle cuts off the apex of the corner. At lights wait behind big vehicles, and let them go ahead around corners.

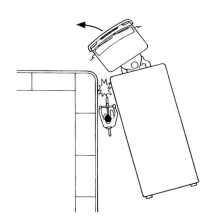

GOOD CYCLING TECHNIQUES

Indicate and communicate

Use big arm movements in plenty of time to let drivers react. Make eye contact. Call out. Use a bell. Thank a helpful manoeuvre with a thumbs-up or the like.

Be well lit at night

Drivers see only lights after dark, not shadows. Reflective strips are a great aid.

Be patient and control your temper

Learning to handle the occasional idiot is part of becoming a true cyclist.

Don't be late

Cycling takes skill, nerve and balance. If you are worried or late, you are putting yourself at risk. Keep your mind on the riding.

Get reasonably fit

Then you can flow with the traffic, not against it, get out of small spaces quicker – and enjoy yourself more.

City Centre and Salford Tour

There's a huge amount packed into just 12km on this ride, with far too many attractions for one day, so just pick one or two to stop at, save the others for another day. Passing, as it does, through the city centre, Sunday is the best day to tackle the route. The traffic is much quieter, and the attractions still open. Manchester's centre is very compact, so it is easy to explore by bike, and the Salford Quays developments make an attractive destination to the west.

Urbis

The extraordinary glass wedge of the Urbis building is home to an exploration of contemporary urban culture and cities of the present and the future. You ride (elevator not bike!) to the top and work your way down through numerous galleries and displays, looking at urban life and design from cities around the world.

The Lowry

The steel clad shapes of the Lowry house the major collection of the work of the painter LS Lowry, who captured images of Manchester and Salford life. The centre also houses two theatres, exhibition spaces, shops, restaurants and bars. It is surrounded by the Salford Quays, once the dock from which the vessels

RIDE INFORMATION

Distance	12 km (7 miles)
Car-free	1km (8%)
Grade	Easy, the route is flat, but navigation needs concentration at times.

Bike
Any bike is fine. Carry a good lock for stopping-off points.

Suitable for children and beginners?
Yes, if they are okay to ride through the city centre

Traffic and surface
Traffic is light on a Sunday, the surface is good all the way round.

Start/finish
Piccadilly station, although it could just as well be Victoria or Deansgate if they are more convenient.

Stations
Any of the city centre stations will do.

Refreshments
All the sites mentioned provide catering, the new museums being good.

What to see
Museums, football and cricket grounds, the Ship Canal and Salford Quays.

Sightseeing information
Most of the museums and galleries currently offer free entry – a fantastic reason, not that an excuse is needed, to visit these fine attractions.

Above: The Imperial War Museum North.
Below: The Lowry.

Castlefield Basin.

Shiny new museum 1.

Shiny new museum 2.

The view from the War Museum Tower.

of the Manchester Ship Canal traded with the world – at one time this was the fourth busiest port in the UK. Across the square from the Lowry is a large shopping centre, while the Lowry Footbridge links the site to that other shining metallic dockside space, the Imperial War Museum North.

Imperial War Museum North
Opened in 2002, the IWM North appears as a series of sculptural forms suggesting a world shattered by war. Inside, the contents focus on how war affects the lives of those it touches. There are exhibitions, a series of audio-visual shows which are projected onto the gallery walls, and collections of artefacts linked to different experiences of war. It is possible to go up to the top of the tower, to look back across the city from a spectacular vantage point. There is also a very nice museum cafe.

Manchester United and Old Trafford
Manchester United is now one of the biggest clubs in the world, and surely Manchester's

most famous export. There is a museum in which you can learn about the history of the club from 1878 to the present day. There is also a tour of the stadium, which lets you visit the parts not normally open to the public. You can sit in the changing rooms, or even pretend you are the manager standing by the dugout shouting at an imaginary referee! The Museum and Tour and shop are open year round. More information at www.manutd.co.uk.

Museum of Science and Industry
This, one of Manchester's most important historic sites, started life as Liverpool Road Station in 1830, and continued as a working rail depot right up until 1975. The museum opened here in 1983 and has gradually expanded to occupy many adjoining historic buildings. The museum houses a vast collection of industrial heritage and artefacts from industries significant in the northwest. These include everything from printing and textiles, to manufacturing and air and space travel. There are regular touring exhibitions and it's all free!! Highly recommended.

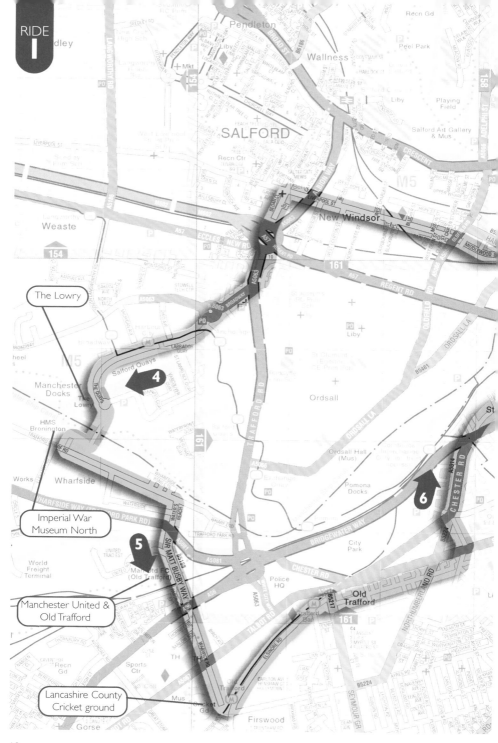

RIDE
1

The Lowry

Imperial War Museum North

Manchester United & Old Trafford

Lancashire County Cricket ground

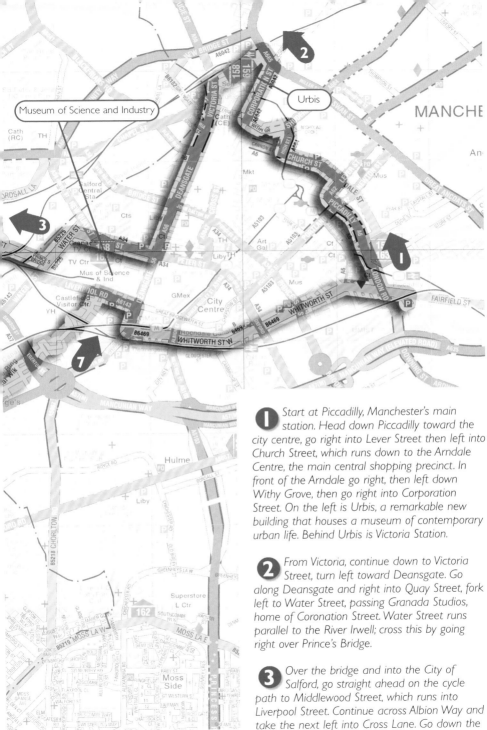

Museum of Science and Industry

Urbis

MANCHE

Start at Piccadilly, Manchester's main station. Head down Piccadilly toward the city centre, go right into Lever Street then left into Church Street, which runs down to the Arndale Centre, the main central shopping precinct. In front of the Arndale go right, then left down Withy Grove, then go right into Corporation Street. On the left is Urbis, a remarkable new building that houses a museum of contemporary urban life. Behind Urbis is Victoria Station.

From Victoria, continue down to Victoria Street, turn left toward Deansgate. Go along Deansgate and right into Quay Street, fork left to Water Street, passing Granada Studios, home of Coronation Street. Water Street runs parallel to the River Irwell; cross this by going right over Prince's Bridge.

Over the bridge and into the City of Salford, go straight ahead on the cycle path to Middlewood Street, which runs into Liverpool Street. Continue across Albion Way and take the next left into Cross Lane. Go down the

19

Below: Installation on the dockside at Salford Quays.

underpass under the roundabout at the start of the M602. Take the path which forks left, to come up by Trafford Road. Turn right into Broadway and at the roundabout take first exit, left, to go past the dockside office developments and along to the Lowry.

4 From outside the Lowry, cross the Manchester Ship Canal on the new Lowry Footbridge and cross to the Imperial War Museum North. Pass to the left of IWMN to join Trafford Wharf Road, where you turn left on the cycle path before turning right into Waters Reach. Cross Wharfside Way and the Bridgewater Canal into Sir Matt Busby Way.

5 Old Trafford is the home of Manchester United, and one of the world's most famous football grounds. Continue past the ground and cross the A56 into Warwick Road. Pass the other 'Old Trafford', this time the Lancashire county cricket ground. At the end of the road is Old Trafford Metro station. Take the path underneath (sign to Altrincham Platform) to join Elsinore Road. Turn left into Elsinore Road, then go across Seymour Grove, going right then left into Stanley Road. Cross Northumberland Road and continue on Stanley Road, then go left into Sudbury Close, across Stretford Road and into East Union Street by a primary school. Turn right onto Chester Road.

6 From Chester Road cross the A56 Bridgewater Way into Ellesmere Street. Go left into Arundel Street, and right into Worsley Street. Go beneath the main road and left onto the Bridgewater Canal; the towpath isn't usable for cycling – please dismount – but a very short walk leads into the Castlefield Basin, where the Bridgewater and Rochdale canals meet.

7 Go over the modern bridge into Castle Street then Duke Street to come out by the Museum of Science and Industry on Liverpool Road. Turn right to take Liverpool Road to Deansgate. Turn right, go under the rail bridge and then left into Whitworth Street. Follow Whitworth Street across Albion Street. The site of the famous Hacienda club (now flats) is on the corner here. Continue along Whitworth Street back to Piccadilly Station.

Old Trafford, home of Manchester United.

Heaton Park

Starting in Manchester's biggest park and crossing into Rochdale and Bury, this ride follows minor roads and off-road tracks on a circuit of real variety. From Heaton Park in Prestwich on the northern edge of the city, the route travels in a loop north, then weaves a path under and over the criss-crossing motorways to discover unexpected lanes and views back across Manchester.

Heaton Park is Manchester's largest, with some 650 acres of green park and woodland, sited north of the city in the Pennine foothills. The Hall is largely as built in the 18th century, although changes were made in the 1820s. It is said to be one of the finest houses of its period in the country. The surrounding parkland became public in 1902 and is claimed to be the largest municipal park in Europe. It is currently undergoing major redevelopment to improve what is already a wide range of attractions. As well the huge amount of open space, you will find a collection of farm and other animals for children, a boating lake, a working tramway at weekends, a golf course, horticultural centre and the site of the Commonwealth Games bowling. You can easily cycle 5km round the park exploring, before setting off on the route.

RIDE INFORMATION

Distance   23km (14 miles)
Car-free   4km (2.5 miles) (14%)
Grade   Medium

Bike   Preferably with knobbly tyres

Suitability for children and beginners?
OK, just be careful on busy Pilsworth Road at the northernmost point

Traffic and surface
Mixed, mostly quiet, 4km off-road

Start/finish
St Margaret's Gate (car park) at Heaton Park, on the A576 Bury Old Road, 8km from city centre

Station
Manchester Victoria in central Manchester is closest, 6km from the start

Refreshments
Three Arrows pub off Old Hall Lane, White Hart Hotel in Birch, Three Arrows Inn on Moss Hall Road, good chip shop on the corner Mount Road/Heywood Road

The bridleway at the perimeter of Heaton Park.

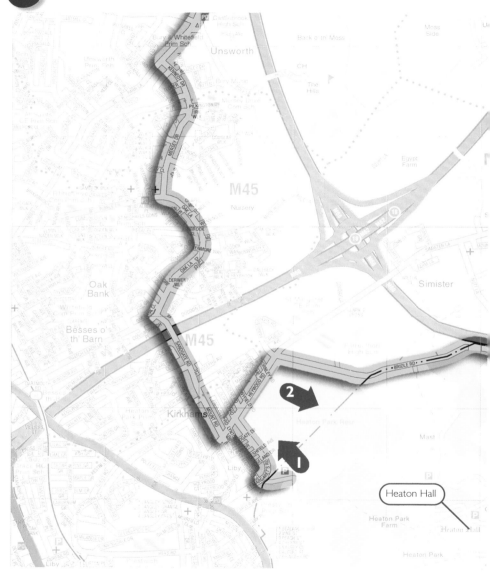

Heaton Hall

1 The route starts at St Margaret's Gate at the northwestern corner of the park, accessed from St Margaret's Road off Bury Old Road. Exiting the park, turn right onto St Margaret's Road, then after 500m right onto Heywood Road.

2 Take the next right, onto the bridleway, Bridle Road, opposite Parrenthorn Road. The bridleway skirts the northern edge of the park, then descends as Old Hall Lane between the park on the right and the M60 motorway on the left.

3 *The track ends when it comes out close to the Three Arrows pub. Turn left here and take the underpass that allows safe passage across the motorway junction. Emerge to join Middleton Road, then turn left uphill on Heywood Old Road. The road climbs to Bowlee then continues towards Birch.*

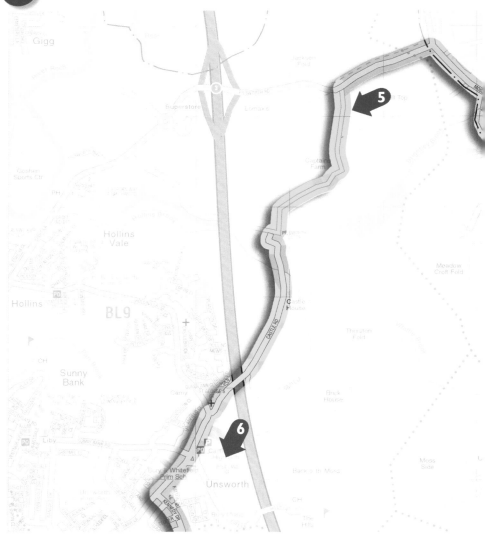

4 At Birch turn left onto Whittle Lane just before the White Hart Hotel. Go over the M62 past the back of Birch motorway services – a possible refreshment stop if you use the access road! Continue, becoming Moss Hall Road, down to a T-junction, where there's another Three Arrows Inn on the right. Turn left, then take the next left at the traffic lights for a short stretch on busy Pilsworth Road.

5 After 500m, turn left off Pilsworth Road for a pleasant little off-road section that marks the start of the return leg. The track at first climbs a little then descends past Captain's Farm. This is the roughest part of the route, and the only stretch which really requires a mountain bike, but it's short, and can be walked if you are on a road bike.

Take a moment to savour the views back

...across Manchester. The path turns into a cobbled road passing Pilsworth Cottages, and climbs again to cross the M60.

6 After crossing the M60, return to suburban Bury. Descend past Castlebrook High School on the left, then a row of shops. Then turn left at a mini-roundabout onto Kennedy Drive/Mersey Drive. At the next T-junction, opposite the Prince Albert pub, turn left onto Oak Lane, then left again at another mini-roundabout into Sandgate Road. This makes our fourth and final motorway crossing and runs into Mount Road. From here go left (chip shop on corner) onto Heywood Road, and right back into St Margaret's Road, to the park gates.

Tandle Hill to Hollins

This very fine, almost entirely off-road route for sturdy bikes, forms a figure-of-eight squeezed between Oldham, Rochdale and Manchester. The paths are good and the views spectacular from Tandle Hill, while the loop north of Hollins includes really good tracks. These two sections are connected by a short stretch on the towpath of the Rochdale Canal.

Tandle Hill Country Park, one of Oldham's oldest country parks, is 110 acres of woodland and grassland with superb views east towards the Pennines and west over the Manchester plain. The name Tandle Hill means 'fire hill'. The area was donated to the people of Royton to mark the end of the 1914-18 war and was officially opened on 6 September 1919. In the early 19th century, at the time of the Peterloo

massacre (when a huge rally for parliamentary reform in Manchester was broken up by the Army with 11 deaths and many casualties), Tandle Hill was the site of political meetings for the local radicals who practised marching and drilling here. Eventually, the woodland was planted to prevent this!

1 *Tandle Hill Country Park main entrance is at the end of Tandle Hill Road off the A671 between Rochdale and Oldham. Start by going back down Tandle Hill Road, turn left and go up the hill towards Summit.*

2 *At Summit turn left just after the post office to join Thornham Old Road. Here the route enters the open space between*

RIDE INFORMATION

Distance	17km (11 miles)
Car-free	15km (9.4 miles) (90%)
Grade	Medium: no major hills and almost all well surfaced

Bike
Mountain bike or hybrid would be best as this route has a high proportion of off-road riding

Suitability for children and beginners?
Good: there should be no problems managing this route

Traffic and surface
90% tracks or towpath with no traffic

Start/finish
The entrance car park at Tandle Hill Country Park, Royton, Oldham, on the A671 between Oldham and Rochdale

Stations
Close to stations at Oldham (4km), Rochdale (3km) and Shaw & Compton (2.5km)

Refreshments
The cafe at Tandle Hill visitor centre is open most weekends; a single pub, the Tandle Hill Tavern, is en route

What to see
Spectacular views from Tandle Hill, Rochdale Canal and good paths around Hopwood Hall

Above: Rochdale Canal at Slattocks. Below: Path through the woods by Hopwood Hall.

Oldham to the south and Rochdale to the north, and being on high ground, the views are excellent. The lane is unsurfaced but fine for riding on; eventually you begin to descend and pass through the few houses and a pub that make up Thornham Fold. The lane goes over the A627(M), and becomes a good fast descent down to the A664 Manchester Road. Cross directly over the road to join the towpath.

3 The Rochdale Canal runs from Rochdale down to the centre of Manchester. Turn left onto it and follow it down past a series of locks, and carefully go through the tight tunnel below the A664 Rochdale Road. Cross over the canal at the next bridge – this is just before the railway bridge which crosses the canal.

4 After crossing the canal pass under the railway bridge. Bear right on a track which links up with Whitegates Road. Take this, then join Rochdale Road and go left. After 200m carefully cross Rochdale Road (sign for Middleton campus of Hopwood College). Here, join a very nice set of tracks on an anticlockwise circuit around Hopwood Hall College. Take the first track on the right, Oaken Bank Road, with Trub Brook to its left. Climb through very nice woodland before emerging into more open farmland and descending to the junction with Stott Lane.

5 Stott Lane first climbs then descends to come out by a school on the left. Turn left to pass in front of the school and behind the houses of Hollins, pick up the very nice rolling

track which returns toward Rochdale Road. Rejoin the outward route and retrace the path, over Rochdale Road, Whitegates Road, and back to the canal. This time, turn right, to continue on the towpath to Stanycliffe.

6 Leave the canal at the first opportunity, going left onto Boarshaw Lane at Stanycliffe. Follow Boarshaw Lane, an industrial estate to the left and fields to the right, before passing under the motorway A627(M). Tandle Hill is now above and to the left.

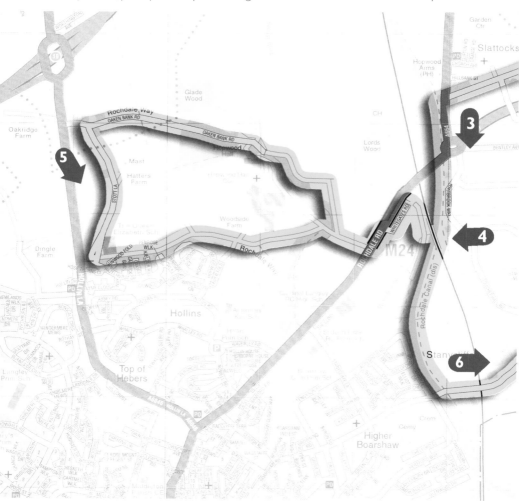

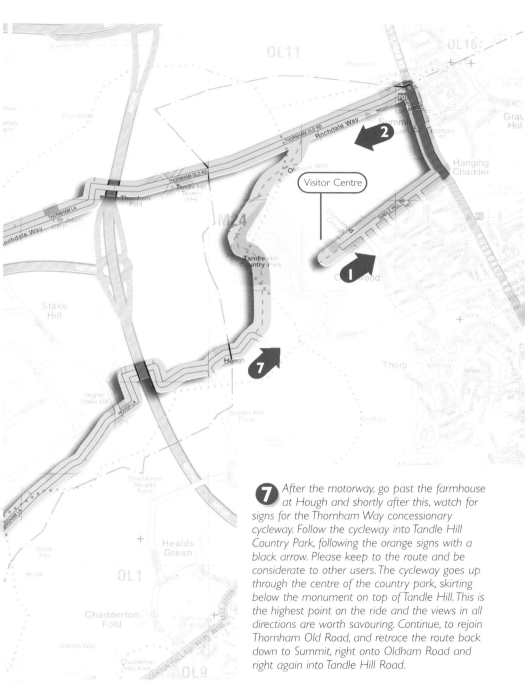

7 After the motorway, go past the farmhouse at Hough and shortly after this, watch for signs for the Thornham Way concessionary cycleway. Follow the cycleway into Tandle Hill Country Park, following the orange signs with a black arrow. Please keep to the route and be considerate to other users. The cycleway goes up through the centre of the country park, skirting below the monument on top of Tandle Hill. This is the highest point on the ride and the views in all directions are worth savouring. Continue, to rejoin Thornham Old Road, and retrace the route back down to Summit, right onto Oldham Road and right again into Tandle Hill Road.

East Manchester Towpaths

From the ultra-modern sports stadia of Sport City to the canals of the 18th century, this short route, which can be done on any bike, explores aspects of Manchester's past and its future. Nearly half of it is on canal towpaths, and there is a halfway snack stop at Daisy Nook Country Park. This ride links with Ride 5, Daisy Nook to Hartshead Pike, and the pair can be combined for a longer day out.

The National Cycling Centre, otherwise known as the Manchester Velodrome, is Britain's best indoor cycle track and has proved to be one of world's fastest. Home to our Olympic and Commonwealth champions,

the track also hosts regular local racing and training sessions and offers introductions to beginners in this most exciting of cycling disciplines. If you would like to hire a bike and give it a go, contact the Manchester Velodrome (tel 0161 223 2244, www.manchestervelodrome.com).

The Ashton Canal was developed in response to the success of the Bridgewater Canal west of Manchester. A group of entrepreneurs saw the potential to bring coal into the city from the east. Opened in 1796 it runs from behind Piccadilly station in Manchester via 18 locks to Fairfield. From

RIDE INFORMATION

Distance   15km (9 miles)
Car-free   7km (4 miles) (45%)
Grade   Easy: mostly towpath with a few small hills out by Daisy Nook

Bike
The towpaths are generally well surfaced, so any bike will do

Suitablity for children and beginners?
Good

Traffic and surface
Short busy sections through Droylsden and Failsworth, with reasonable surfaces

Start/finish
Stuart Street, close to National Cycling Centre

Station
Manchester Victoria (4km)

Refreshments
Fast food and supermarket at the start, Daisy Nook visitor centre at the halfway point

What to see
Sport City (completely redesigned for the 2002 Commonwealth Games, including the National Cycling Centre and the City of Manchester Stadium, now home to Manchester City FC); Ashton and Rochdale canals; Daisy Nook Country Park in the borough of Oldham, was designated in 1976, but has been a place of recreation for locals since the mid-19th century. Its lakes, canals and woodland are popular with walkers, horse-riders, cyclists and anglers. The John Howarth Countryside Centre, named after a local benefactor, serves information, food and drinks, and has toilets.

Ashton Canal and the National Cycling Centre.

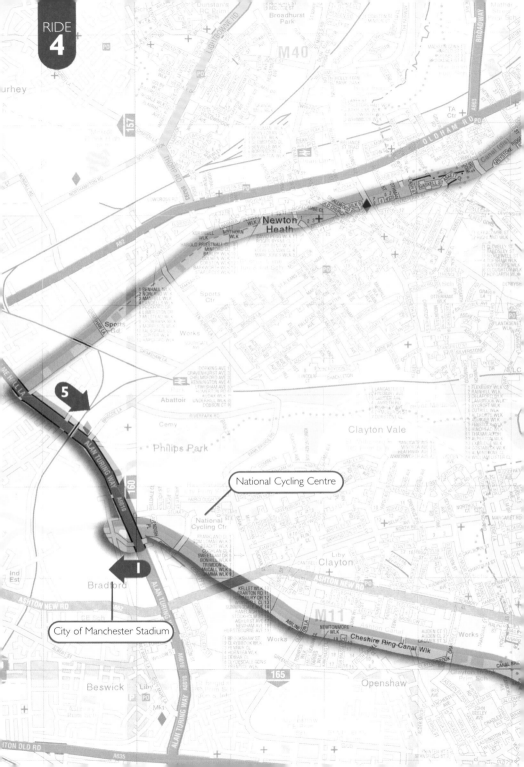

National Cycling Centre

City of Manchester Stadium

Daisy Nook Visitor Centre

there a number of short arms split off to serve different areas, including Daisy Nook.

The Rochdale Canal became the first complete Trans Pennine Canal in 1804, when different sections were finally joined together. However, less than 40 years later, the Manchester & Leeds Railway opened and the canals struggled to compete. The last working boat crossed the Pennines in 1937. The canals fell into decline and disrepair and it was only in the 1980s and '90s that restoration work began on some stretches. In 2002, after years of work at a cost of millions of pounds, the Rochdale Canal was completely re-opened, virtually 200 years after its original opening.

1 *Start at the junction of Gibbon Street and Alan Turing Way at the heart of Manchester's Sport City. From Gibbon Street turn right and go 100m to reach the entrance to the towpath of the Ashton Canal. Turn right onto the towpath by an old lock-keepers' cottage. Head*

out along this 3.5km stretch of towpath passing close to the Velodrome. The towpath is initially narrow, but soon improves and widens. All the locks are conveniently numbered, so this section begins at Lock 7 and passes the Strawberry Duck pub on the opposite bank, by Lock 13. At Lock 18 the canal widens to form a basin.

2 *After the canal basin and just before Bridge 17 (the bridges have numbers too), leave the towpath by taking the ramp off right that goes up to join Market Street in Fairfield. Turn left onto Market Street and cross the canal. Follow Market Street through Droylsden. After 1.5km the road bends 90 degrees left and passes over a railway line. The landscape opens up now, with hills to the right and the Medlock Valley to the left. Follow Lumb Lane over the M60 motorway. Where the road next turns sharp right, instead, carry straight on down the hill: the entrance to Daisy Nook Country Park is immediately on the right.*

Best to stay sober on the
Rochdale Canal towpath.

74 **Drunken Bridge**

3 Daisy Nook makes an ideal halfway stopping point. The park is also the starting point for Ride 5 to Hartshead Pike.

Continuing with Ride 4, leave the visitor centre, turn right and go down the hill passing a garden centre on the left. The lane twists and turns and climbs back over the M60 before dropping towards Failsworth.

Stay on Ashton Road, pass a large old mill on the right, then immediately after the road bends round to the right rejoin the towpath by going down some steps on the left.

4 These steps lead down to the Rochdale Canal. The towpath is in very good condition, being wide and well surfaced. Follow the canal for 3.5km from Failsworth down through Newton Heath. We stay on the towpath as far as Lock 77. (The canal continues right into Manchester city centre where it connects with the Bridgewater Canal at Castlefield.)

5 At Lock 77 leave the canal and turn left onto Hulme Hall Lane. Follow the segregated cycle path from here into Alan Turing Way, and then back to the starting point.

Daisy Nook to Hartshead Pike

This short but hilly mountain bike route tours the industrial heritage of the Medlock Valley and has views from Hartshead Pike right across Manchester and beyond. It is not a long ride but it packs a lot into a few kilometres. This ride is easily joined to Ride 4, East Manchester Towpaths, for a longer day out.

Park Bridge, beside the River Medlock, is an extraordinary place that seems to have been home to every form of industry. The first ironworks were founded here in the 1780s, the village thrived and by the mid-19th century grew to have coal mines, cotton

and steel mills. The village had a school, church and its own railway station and canal link. But by the 1960s, the factories had closed and now just the museum and a handful of ruins remain.

From Hartshead Pike, 287m above sea level, it is possible to see the city centre city 13km away, the Welsh hills 110km away and Winter Hill above Lever Park, 33km distant. The present tower was built to mark the wedding of the Prince of Wales and Princess Alexandra in 1863, but the site has been an important hilltop beacon since the 16th century.

RIDE INFORMATION

Distance	14km (9 miles)
Car-free	4km (2.5miles) (30%)
Grade	Difficult
Bike	Mountain bike recommended

Suitability for children and beginners?
Not recommended

Traffic and surface
Traffic light, surface mixed, can be muddy in places

Start/finish
Daisy Nook Country Park, small car park at the John Haworth Countryside Centre

Stations
Ashton-under-Lyne 3km from the start

Refreshments
At Daisy Nook Country Park and Park Bridge

What to see
Daisy Nook Country Park, Medlock Valley (the visitor centre explains the history, flora and fauna of the area, and there is a tearoom and art space), views from Hartshead Pike

Its a long climb but worth it – Hartshead Pike

Above: Park Bridge in the Medlock Valley.
Below: Sharing the trails at Daisy Nook.

1 Start at the John Haworth Countryside Centre in Daisy Nook Country Park. Head along the well-marked path towards the country park. After crossing the River Medlock take the path which turns right, up through the woods. The path joins the Fairbottom Branch Canal path; cross Knott Lane and continues beside the canal, towards the Ashton Road, A627. A small tunnel carries the path under the main road and continues through the woods on the other side, running parallel to the road. Join Park Bridge Road.

2 Turn right onto Park Bridge Road, take the left fork (staying on Park Bridge Road); there is a short length of old cobbled road here. Up the hill on the left is Park Bridge, make the short sharp climb to get there.

3 Park Bridge is a fascinating old industrial complex, explained by the Medlock Valley visitor centre. From there continue up to Dean Terrace, then go left and continue for 1 km to Alt and the main road.

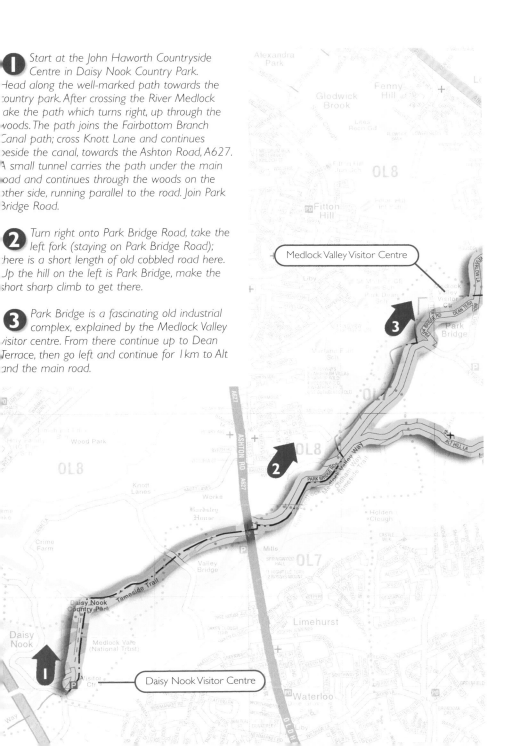

Medlock Valley Visitor Centre

Daisy Nook Visitor Centre

RIDE 5

4 Turn right onto the main road and, after a short descent, take the first left into Lees New Road. After just over 1km turn right into Knowls Lane and begin the long climb towards Hartshead Pike (take it steady!); soon take the right fork by St Agnes Primary School into Lane Head Road and go up up up . . . The next right leads to Hartshead Pike. Having arrived, savour the view from the Pike – fantastic in all directions.

The view from Hartshead Pike.

5 Continue along the track below the Pike, go through a gate to join Lily Lanes and turn right. At first the track is steep with rocky steps, but it soon becomes easier. Lily Lanes is a long and fast descent; halfway down turn right and continue to the junction with Lees Road.

6 Continue straight across and climb 1km to the tiny village of Alt Hill. Then drop back into the Medlock Valley to rejoin Park Bridge Road. Go left and turn into the off-road path to follow the outward route back to Daisy Nook.

Hartshead Pike

Reddish Vale and Canals

Starting from Reddish Vale this ride takes a long loop clockwise along canals and riverside paths to make an unexpectedly green and traffic-free route, squeezed in between the townships of eastern Manchester, Tameside and Stockport.

Ashton Canal

Construction began on the Ashton Canal between Manchester and Ashton-under-Lyne in 1794. The canal runs from Ashton-under-Lyne to Manchester. It connects with the Rochdale Canal near Piccadilly at its western end, and the Huddersfield Narrow just east of Ashton.

Ride 4 also uses the Ashton Canal, and could be combined with this ride to make a 35km figure of eight.

Peak Forest Canal

Running south from the Ashton Canal, the Peak Forest connects the towns on the eastern edge of Greater Manchester; Ashton, Dukinfield, Hyde, Romiley, Marple and New Mills, before heading toward the Peak District. It has been well restored and has a wide towpath good for riding on.

Debdale Park

Debdale Park and Gorton upper and lower reservoirs are at the eastern end of the Fallowfield Loop Line. The Loop Line can be used to access the route at this point if riding from south/west Manchester. It feeds in to the western end of the park and makes riding across town a real pleasure compared with battling with traffic.

RIDE INFORMATION

Distance 20km (13 miles)
Car-free 15km (9.4 miles) (75%)
Grade Medium, the ride is largely flat, but there are a few short climbs, some off-road trails and rough surfaces.

Bike
Mountain Bike recommended

Suitable for children and beginners?
A high proportion of off-road riding, but quite hard going at times as the surfaces can be hard work. One to build up to

Start/finish
Reddish Vale visitor centre

Traffic and surface
One short busy road stretch. Surfaces can be rough, but always okay for mountain bikes

Stations
Reddish South is closest

Refreshments
There is a cafe at the animal centre on Reddish Vale Road, just up the hill from the visitor centre. Otherwise nothing on route, but plenty of places in the towns close to the route

What to see
Historic canals, River Tame

Above: Feeding the birds – Reddish Vale Visitor Centre.
Below: The Junction of the Ashton and High Peak canals.

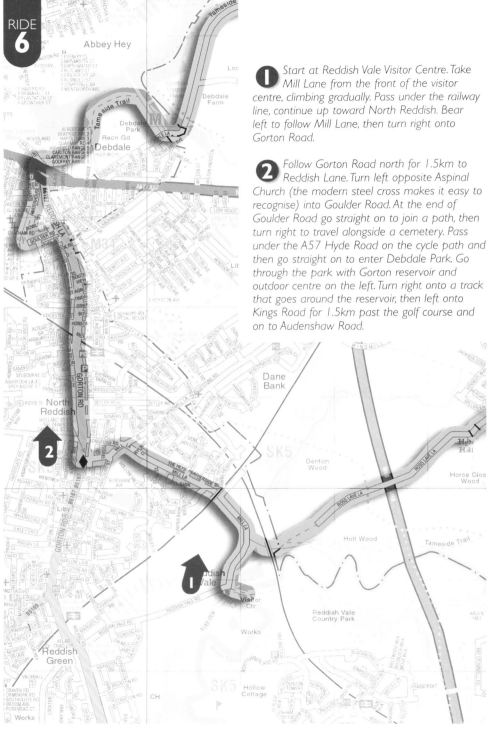

1 Start at Reddish Vale Visitor Centre. Take Mill Lane from the front of the visitor centre, climbing gradually. Pass under the railway line, continue up toward North Reddish. Bear left to follow Mill Lane, then turn right onto Gorton Road.

2 Follow Gorton Road north for 1.5km to Reddish Lane. Turn left opposite Aspinal Church (the modern steel cross makes it easy to recognise) into Goulder Road. At the end of Goulder Road go straight on to join a path, then turn right to travel alongside a cemetery. Pass under the A57 Hyde Road on the cycle path and then go straight on to enter Debdale Park. Go through the park with Gorton reservoir and outdoor centre on the left. Turn right onto a track that goes around the reservoir, then left onto Kings Road for 1.5km past the golf course and on to Audenshaw Road.

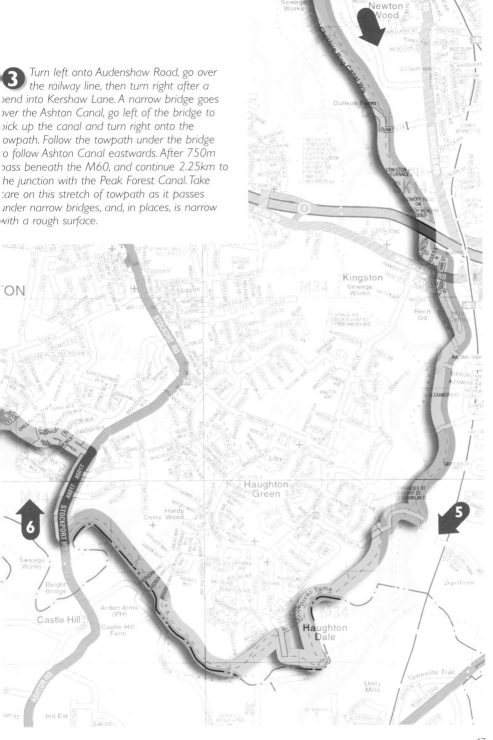

3 Turn left onto Audenshaw Road, go over the railway line, then turn right after a bend into Kershaw Lane. A narrow bridge goes over the Ashton Canal, go left of the bridge to pick up the canal and turn right onto the towpath. Follow the towpath under the bridge to follow Ashton Canal eastwards. After 750m pass beneath the M60, and continue 2.25km to the junction with the Peak Forest Canal. Take care on this stretch of towpath as it passes under narrow bridges, and, in places, is narrow with a rough surface.

4 At Ashton-under-Lyne leave the Ashton Canal and turn right to join the Peak Forest Canal. The Peak Forest heads south, initially running high above the River Tame, which is down to the right. The towpath on this stretch is wide and well surfaced, and the canal has a very pleasant rural feel to it. After 3km, approach Hyde passing under the M67. Go under the A57 Manchester Road bridge. This is a 'roving bridge' where the towpath changes from one side to the other, designed so that horses could cross without having to be detached from their tow ropes. After a further 1km the canal passes under another roving bridge as the towpath changes sides yet again.

5 Just before an iron footbridge leave the towpath, going down to the right, to descend a long flight of steps to Gibraltar Lane. Follow the lane down through a wooded valley and across the River Tame. Go immediately left on to a path following the Trans Pennine Trail (TPT) signs downstream through riverside meadows at Haughton Dale. Stay north of Tame on this 3km-long section of trail which leads to Stockport Road.

6 Turn right on to Stockport Road, go up the hill, then left into Yew Tree Road. Turn right off the road into a path opposite Hodnet Walk (TPT sign). Walk this short 100m stretch to reach the path which goes down to Ross Lave Lane. Ross Lave Lane is a rough track that leads up through fields with good views to hills in the distance, over the M60, then begins a nice descent back to Reddish Vale. Go under the viaduct, around the lake and rejoin Mill Lane. Turn left to return to the visitor centre.

Trans Pennine Trail in Haughton Dale.

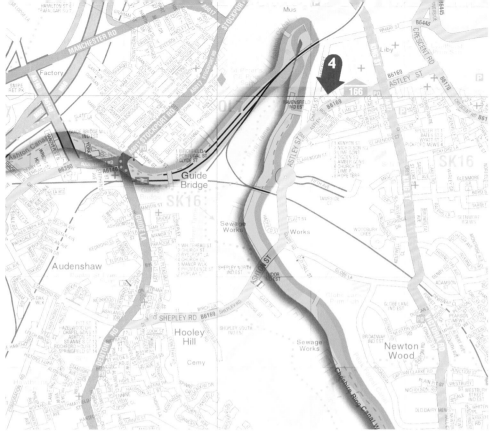

Reddish Vale and Loop Line

Reddish Vale is a valuable green space surrounded by Manchester, Stockport and Tameside. Happily, it also features a disused railway line, which has been converted into an excellent trail. The River Tame flows through the park as well, and at its southern end joins the River Goyt to form the Mersey. On the return this ride uses a small part of the excellent Fallowfield Loop Line, which, if time allows, is well worth exploring further.

The River Mersey is fed by two smaller rivers; the Tame, which flows south from Saddleworth Moor, and the Goyt, which comes east from near Buxton in Derbyshire. At Reddish Vale they meet to become the Mersey, and this then flows west, down the estuary past Liverpool to the Irish Sea.

The MidShires Way, which passes through Reddish Vale, is a lesser-known long-distance footpath and bridleway through middle England. Around 225 miles long it connects the Ridgeway in the south with the Trans Pennine Trail and then the Pennine Way/Pennine Bridleway in the north. When these trails are all complete and signed there will be the exciting possibility of a ride the length of England. Brief guides and maps can be tracked down, although at the time of writing, the trail does have a low profile.

1 *Start at Reddish Vale Visitor Centre, found at the end of Reddish Vale Road, close to Reddish South Station. From in front of the centre go down beside the lake and over the bridge across the River Tame. Pick up the Trans Pennine Trail signs which lead to the right across the meadow and up toward the disused rail line. A set of steps leads up to the level of the disused railway line, turn right. Follow the line south through cuttings and woodland, down to the right*

RIDE INFORMATION

Distance 11km (7 miles)
Car-free 4km (2.5 miles) (36%)
Grade Easy

Bike
Mountain Bike recommended

Suitable for children and beginners?
Yes, the trails are not difficult and the roads are relatively quiet.

Traffic and surface
The trails are well drained, the roughest part is Nelstrop Road North

Start and Finish
Reddish Vale Visitor Centre

Stations
Reddish South

Refreshments
There is a cafe at the animal centre on Reddish Vale Road, just up the hill from the visitor centre

What to see
The Country Park, the source of the River Mersey, Fallowfield Loop Line

The trail in Reddish Vale.

The source of the River Mersey.   Which way out of here?

are a golf course, meadows and the River Tame snaking its way toward the junction with the River Goyt where it forms the River Mersey.

2 The cycleway here forms part of the Trans Pennine Trail, and also the lesser known MidShires Way, a long-distance route which runs north-south through the heart of the Midlands. The trail here is very popular, with lots of families and horses using it, so please do be considerate. The path drops down to the road at the southern end of the park. Turn right and cross the Tame on Tiviot Way, then immediately go right and down to the riverside, under Tiviot Way, and follow the river downstream.

3 At the southern point of the park a small diversion is worth making before heading back north. Go left, under the M60, to see the confluence of the Rivers Tame and Goyt where they form the Mersey. There is an interesting artwork marking the spot. Partly designed by local community groups it bears the phrase: 'Water is life and heaven's gift, here Rivers Goyt and Tame become Mersey, flowing clear from Stockport to the Sea'. Turn round and go back over the Tame, head up to the road at Penny Lane. Turn right, go under Tiviot Way, and go right again into Woodhall Fields (cycle path signed North Reddish). A good path follows the edge of the fields into woods and up to Reddish Road.

4 Cross Reddish Road into Greg Street. Follow Greg Street for 800m then turn left (sign for White Hill Industrial Estate) into Broadstone Hall Road South. As the road goes round to left, bear right, staying on Broadstone Hall Road South to go under railway bridge. Cross into Broadstone Hall Road North. At the next junction go left then right into Marbury Road and take the second left into Nelstrop Road North.

5 Nelstrop Road North is a rough track which passes through open space between Reddish and Levenshulme. It connects with the fantastic Fallowfield Loop Line (see information in Introduction), which carves a great traffic-free arc through south Manchester. Although this route only uses a very short stretch it is well worth exploring in both directions at greater length.

6 The Loop Line currently runs up to Debdale, but take the first available exit, to Longford Road West, and go left on it to North Reddish (where there are shops/pubs etc).
Cross Gorton Road into Longford Road, and continue into the quiet Mill Lane. Pass under a rail bridge and descend quickly back to the Visitor Centre.

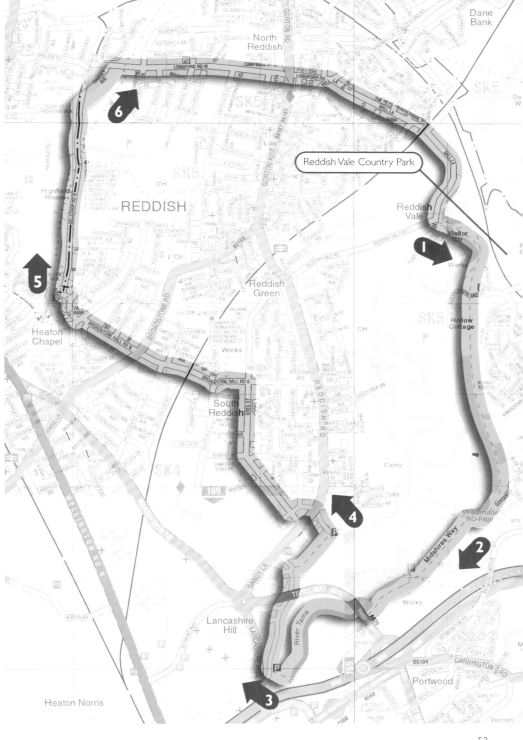

Reddish Vale Country Park

Mersey Valley Riverside Trails

This short route is unique in having so much riverside path to enjoy. The River Mersey is usually associated with Liverpool, yet its waters are also an important feature of Trafford and south Manchester. The meadows either side create a green corridor just a few miles south of Manchester city centre, which is great for traffic-free cycling and is now part of the Trans Pennine Trail. The water parks are relatively new yet they have become important havens for wildlife, and the entire area is managed for flora and fauna and peaceful recreation.

This route shares a starting point with Ride 9 out to Dunham Park, so you can mix and match your riding.

Sale and Chorlton water parks

Both Mersey Valley water parks were created in the early 1970s. Gravel extraction for the construction of the motorways left huge pits, which were then flooded to form the lakes. These are very popular with anglers, sailors and ducks, and the surrounding parks are great for walking and cycling.

Simon's Bridge

This iron bridge dates from 1901 and is the easterly turnaround point of the route. It has always been an important Mersey crossing point; the ford (of Ford Lane) was here, and in medieval times it is thought that packhorses carried their loads into Lancashire this way.

RIDE INFORMATION

Distance   14km (9 miles)
Car-free   12km (7.5 miles) (85%)
Grade   Easy

Bike
Mountain bike recommended

Suitability for children and beginners?
Good

Traffic and surface
Mostly off-road. The paths are good but wet/muddy in places after prolonged rain

Start/finish
Mersey Valley visitor centre in Sale Water Park (see also Ride 9). If cycling to the start from the north, approach via Jackson's

Bridge from Chorlton-cum-Hardy; from the south, avoid the M60 J6 by taking the cycle path from Clarendon Crescent in Sale, then go under the motorway and around Sale Water Park to arrive at the visitor centre. Simon's Bridge, at the turnaround point, is an alternative starting point - see Stations

Stations
Trafford Park 3km north of the start; East Didsbury 1.5km east of Simon's Bridge at point 6

Refreshments
Pubs at Jackson's Bridge and by the weir at point 5

What to see
Lakes, river, wildlife

Above: River Mersey and grass munching geese.
Below: Turn left, or right, or go straight on.

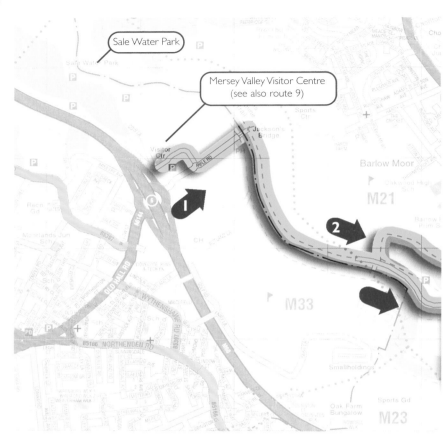

Sale Water Park

Mersey Valley Visitor Centre
(see also route 9)

Barlow Moor

M21

M33

M23

1 Leave the Mersey Valley visitor centre car park and turn left to Rifle Road. At Jackson's Bridge, where there is a popular riverside pub, the Jackson's Boat Inn, cross the river on the narrow bridge – don't try to ride off the north side as there are steep steps. Turn right and join the Trans Pennine Trail (TPT) as it follows the north bank of the Mersey.

2 After 1km you will come to a gate with a turning into Chorlton Water Park on the left. The route returns that way so for now continue on the riverbank path, which becomes a surfaced lane. Cross the next bridge over the river and follow the lane down towards the M60 J5.

3 At the end of the lane follow the TPT sign, turning left to ride on the cycle path beside Princess Road, turn right and cross the road. The next section sounds complicated but on the ground it isn't difficult to navigate as you head to rejoin the riverside upstream.

4 After crossing Princess Road follow the cycle path back over the Mersey, and take the slip road off to the left beneath the motorway. Turn left (signed TPT Didsbury/Stockport) and enter another off-road section in Kenworthy Lane Woods. (Note the TPT is marked with blue signs on the road sections and small green arrows on the off-road sections.)

nice trail runs through the woods parallel to ne M60; take care in the wet on the little rooden bridge. Exit the woods to cross Palatine oad at a toucan crossing.

5 Pass Northenden Weir (built to secure the water supply for the mills which used to e here). Join Mill Lane then Boat Lane before urning left into Ford Lane. Pass beneath the M60 once again, and follow the lane alongside ne riverbank then between sports fields. Recross ne river on Simon's Bridge to regain the north ank of the Mersey.

6 On the north side of the river turn left and follow the riverbank back downstream. Here the Mersey meanders with broad sweeping bends. After 1km pass beneath the M60 again, follow the river north once more towards West Didsbury, then under Princes Parkway to return to Chorlton Water Park.

7 Turn right to leave the riverbank for a circuit of this popular landscaped water park. Follow the good path round and back to the riverside track. Turn right to continue, following the Mersey downstream and return to Jackson's Bridge and cross it back to the visitor centre.

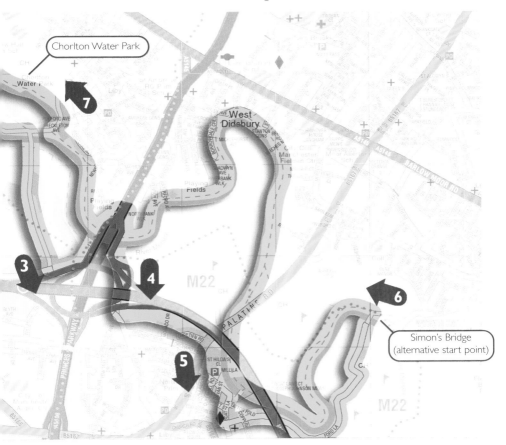

Mersey Valley to Dunham Park

This route takes the rider from the Mersey Valley west along the riverside, then heads south across Carrington Moss before calling at Dunham Park. It scores highly for being largely on well-surfaced off-road paths – on one option the only place to see cars is Dunham Park car park – giving a sense of peace and escape on green paths beneath the roadways. Links to stations are included to give ideas for shortening the route.

This ride shares its start/finish points with Ride 8, Mersey Valley Trails, for other route combinations.

Dunham Massey, originally built in the early 18th century, is a Georgian house that was extensively refurbished in the early 20th century to create one of Britain's finest Edwardian interiors. Outside is also one of the North West's finest gardens as well as a 200-acre park inhabited by hundreds of deer. To visit the hall (and cafe) you are asked to leave bikes at the cycle stands in the car park, as there is no cycling in the grounds. Admission prices (2003): house & garden adult/child/family £5.80/£2.90/£14.50. House or garden only adult/child

RIDE INFORMATION

Distance
30km (19 miles) for the full round trip. Start/finish at Urmston station 24km (15 miles). Finish at Navigation Road 14km (9 miles), or 17km (11 miles) depending on the start
Car-free   10km (6 miles) (33%)
Grade
Medium/easy: the tracks are good, the roads are quiet, and there are no hills. The full route is quite long, the shorter options make it easier

Bike
The off-road sections are well-surfaced so any bike with good strong wheels/tyres should be OK

Suitability for children and beginners?
The tracks are fine, but the full round trip may prove too far for young children and beginners

Traffic and surface
Traffic is light, the off-road sections are on the Trans Pennine Trail (TPT) and are generally well maintained, but cross Carrington Lane with caution as cars here are leaving the motorway spur at high speed

Start/finish
Mersey Valley visitor centre, which serves Sale Water Park and the surrounding green space either side of the River Mersey. The visitor centre is very close to M60 J6; just take Rifle Road north from the motorway junction and the first left into the centre car park.

To ride to the start come up Old Hall Road from Sale, or head south from Manchester, through Chorlton-cum-Hardy and join the route at Jackson Bridge. If travelling by train the best approach is to go to Urmston station and follow the directions (see 2a), to join the route at

Top: The trail passes under the Bridgewater Canal. Below: New bridge over the River Mersey.

point 3. The visitor centre is also the start for Route 8, Mersey Valley trails

Stations
Urmston and Navigation Road are closest and can be used as alternative start/finishes (see above)

Refreshments
Pubs: the Jackson's Bridge Inn near the start, the Axe and Cleaver in Dunham Town, the Rope and Anchor in Dunham Woodhouses, plus a drinks stall and cafe at Dunham Massey (for the cafe you are asked to leave bikes at the cycle stands in the car park, as there is no cycling in the National Trust grounds) (The visitor centre is also the start for Ride 8, Mersey Valley Trails.)

What to see
The River Mersey, Mersey Valley, Dunham Massey park and house (NT)

£3.80/£1.90. See www.nationaltrust.org.uk for opening times and more details.

Trans Pennine Trail (TPT); see separate section on major routes and trails in the area. As with all such trails be considerate toward other users, especially walkers who may not hear you approaching from behind.

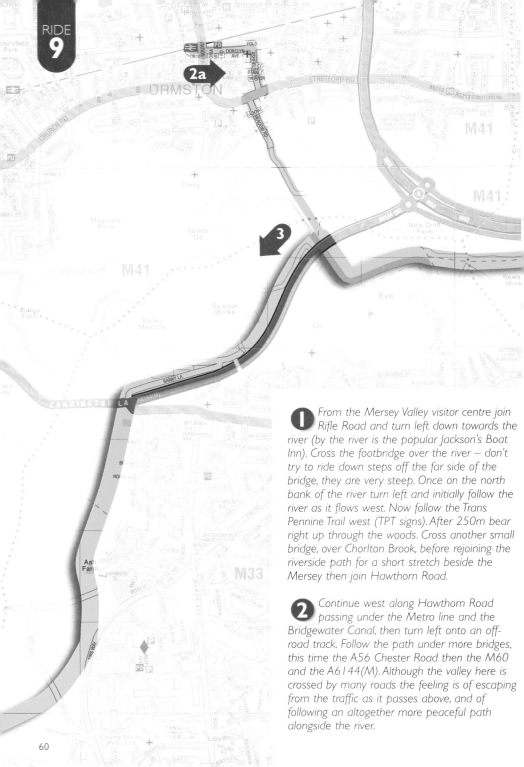

1 From the Mersey Valley visitor centre join Rifle Road and turn left down towards the river (by the river is the popular Jackson's Boat Inn). Cross the footbridge over the river – don't try to ride down steps off the far side of the bridge, they are very steep. Once on the north bank of the river turn left and initially follow the river as it flows west. Now follow the Trans Pennine Trail west (TPT signs). After 250m bear right up through the woods. Cross another small bridge, over Chorlton Brook, before rejoining the riverside path for a short stretch beside the Mersey then join Hawthorn Road.

2 Continue west along Hawthorn Road passing under the Metro line and the Bridgewater Canal, then turn left onto an off-road track. Follow the path under more bridges, this time the A56 Chester Road then the M60 and the A6144(M). Although the valley here is crossed by many roads the feeling is of escaping from the traffic as it passes above, and of following an altogether more peaceful path alongside the river.

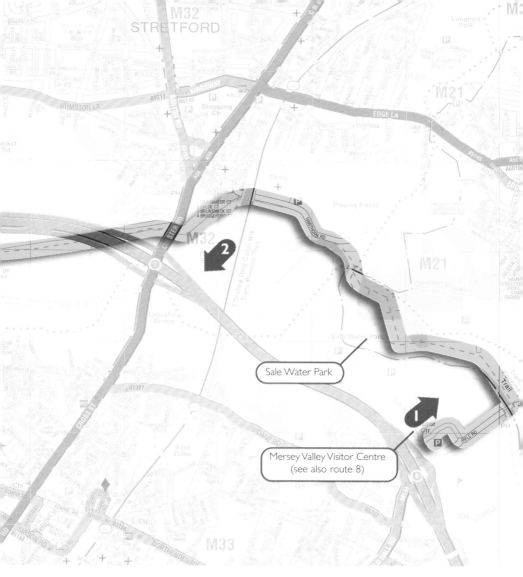

Sale Water Park

Mersey Valley Visitor Centre
(see also route 8)

2a *Alternative start from Urmston station. From the station turn right onto Station Road, then take the first left onto Higher Road and second right to Ashfield Road. At the junction with Stretford Road dogleg right into Meadow Road, follow this all the way down, past the sports ground on the right, to join the main route by the River Mersey at point 3.*

3 *After passing under the A6144(M) cross the Mersey once again on the Trans Pennine Trail bridge and follow the path which runs parallel to the A6144(M), leaving the Mersey as it continues west towards Liverpool. Cross Carrington Lane with caution, as cars are leaving the motorway spur at high speed. Just a few metres down on the right go off-road again. The TPT signs are generally very reliable in giving directions, but by Ash Farm be sure to go left then right at successive T-junctions.*

4 Rejoin the road at Woodcote Road, at the next junction go left towards Broadheath then right into Dairyhouse Lane, follow this past industrial estates to the next T-junction (with Black Moss Road). Go straight over and join another off-road section of old railway line (TPT).

5 Here, the route heads out into the open country between Manchester and Merseyside, and this path goes directly to Warrington (14km) via Lymm (7km). Follow the path west for just over 1km, and pass under the first road bridge (School Lane), then immediately after the bridge go up the steps on the left to join School Lane heading south. Cross a narrow bridge over the Bridgewater Canal to enter Dunham town, the Axe and Cleaver pub on the left. At the next junction turn right, and the next left takes you to Dunham Massey.

6 On leaving the park go left onto Woodhouse Lane which passes under the Bridgewater Canal. At Dunham Woodhouses, go straight on where the road bears left, beside the Rope and Anchor pub. After 100m rejoin the TPT and turn right (signed Altrincham), (turning left gives a 4km ride to Lymm).

7 From here the TPT is a well-surfaced path, with separate sections for horses on one side, and walkers and cyclists on the other. After 1km pass the School Lane bridge, to rejoin the route and return the way it came out, in straightforward fashion.

7a An alternative ending for a shorter ride is to join Atlantic Street at point 5 and head for Navigation Road station.

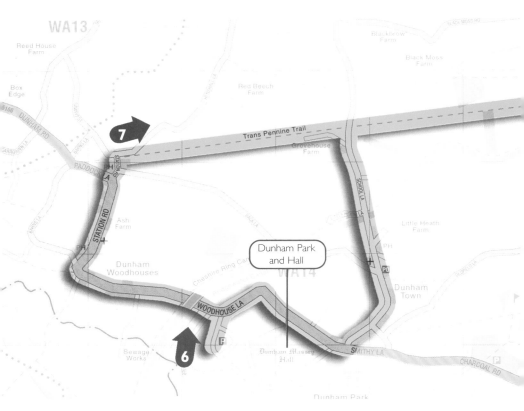

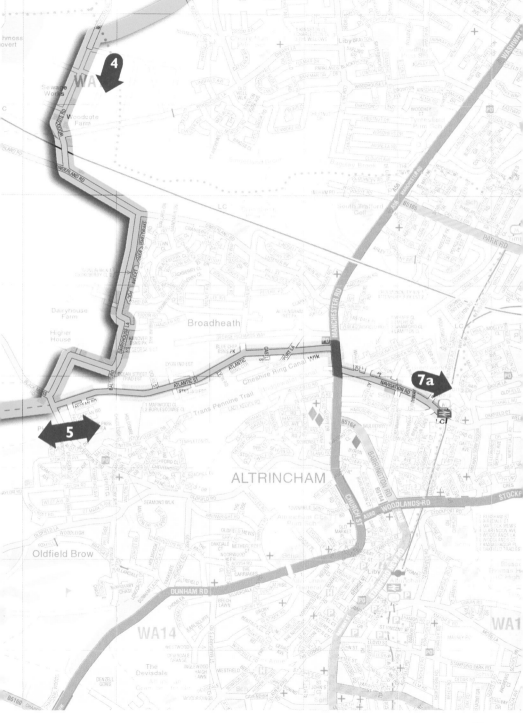

Irwell Valley Trail

The River Irwell carves a wedge of green space dividing Manchester to the east from Salford to the west and providing a fantastic piece of riding so close to the heart of these cities. The route of the old East Lancashire Railway line provides an excellent trail from which to use any bike to explore what is a little-known area, running from Salford up the Irwell Valley to Radcliffe between Bolton and Bury. The route is traffic-free for 10km (20km return), from near Kersal all the way to Radcliffe. Navigating is straightforward, as the main trail is wide and well used, although there are many side-turnings which can be explored as alternatives.

Either side of the valley the roads are busy and less attractive for cycling, so this route goes out and back the same way. If you are used to driving across the valley on the M60, exploring it at a different pace will come as a pleasant surprise. The northern end of the route connects with Ride 11, the Bury Circular, allowing you to mix and match rides if you wish.

At old Ringley Road station you can still see the platform and the line of the tracks. A plaque explains that the East Lancashire Railway opened on 25 September 1846 when two locomotives and 33 carriages travelled from Clifton Junction to Bury. The line closed finally in 1960s and was developed as an urban nature trail in the early 1970s.

RIDE INFORMATION

Distance	26km round trip (16 miles)
Car-free	20km (12.5 miles) (75%)
Grade	Easy: flat and mostly traffic free
Bike	Any sturdy bike

Suitability for children and beginners?
Good: nothing to worry about, being out-and-back makes it easy to turn around at any point

Traffic and surface
Light traffic at the south end of the route, once off-road the surface is generally good, but is sometimes muddy under the trees

Start/finish
Salford Crescent station beside the campus of the University of Salford, 2km from the Manchester city centre

Stations
Nearest to the northern end is Moses Gate, 5km west towards Bolton, allowing you to take the train back to the start/finish, although it is hardly worth it

Refreshments
At the shopping park at the north end of route

What to see
A fascinating area surrounded by industry and development on all sides.

The railway has long since gone, leaving a fine arc of green space ideal for nature and recreation

The trail north of the M60.

Above: Ringley Road crosses over the ride.
Left: This is part of Sustrans National Route 6.

If cycling back to the start, it is worthwhile detouring to explore the open space that lies left (east) of the route just after crossing the M60. Here are lovely trails and an attractive lake that is a haven for wildlife, just metres from the traffic thundering along the M60. Discovering little spots like this is a bonus of exploring by bike. It's easy to pick up the route again, since it is the major trail through the valley, and to the west the river prevents straying too far. Eventually you come to point 3, from where it is just a short road ride back to the start.

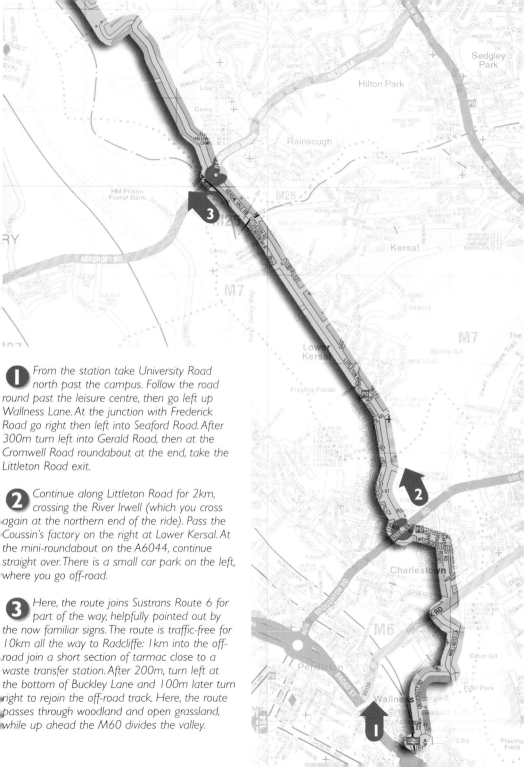

1 From the station take University Road north past the campus. Follow the road round past the leisure centre, then go left up Wallness Lane. At the junction with Frederick Road go right then left into Seaford Road. After 300m turn left into Gerald Road, then at the Cromwell Road roundabout at the end, take the Littleton Road exit.

2 Continue along Littleton Road for 2km, crossing the River Irwell (which you cross again at the northern end of the ride). Pass the Coussin's factory on the right at Lower Kersal. At the mini-roundabout on the A6044, continue straight over. There is a small car park on the left, where you go off-road.

3 Here, the route joins Sustrans Route 6 for part of the way, helpfully pointed out by the now familiar signs. The route is traffic-free for 10km all the way to Radcliffe: 1km into the off-road join a short section of tarmac close to a waste transfer station. After 200m, turn left at the bottom of Buckley Lane and 100m later turn right to rejoin the off-road track. Here, the route passes through woodland and open grassland, while up ahead the M60 divides the valley.

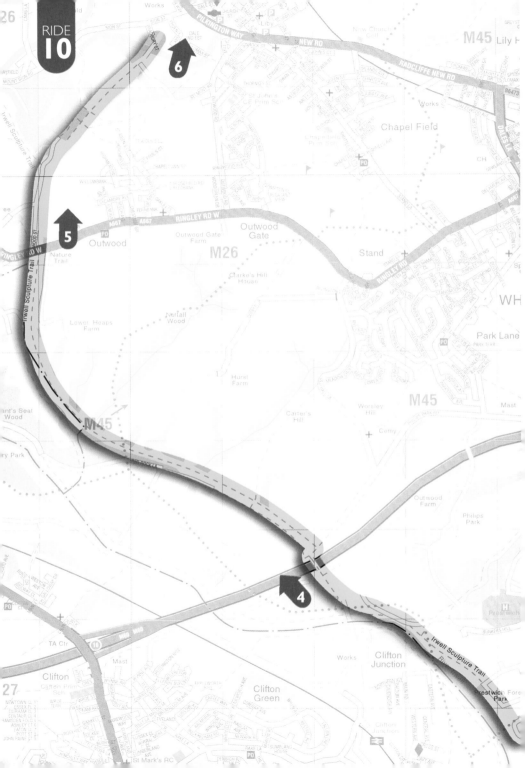

The northern end of the ride, coming into Radcliffe.

4 Cross the M60 on a narrow footbridge. North of the motorway the route follows the line of the old East Lancashire Railway, through what is now quite mature woodland. The surface is generally good but muddy in places after rain. The line of the path is unmistakable and couldn't be easier to follow, just keep going in a straight line!

5 After 2km the path passes through the site of the old Ringley Road station. The next landmark is the massive structure of the bridge which carries Ringley Road over the trail. Continue under this towards the northern end of the route.

6 After 13km the route finally crosses back over the River Irwell, this time on a large traffic-free bridge. Coming off the northern end of the bridge brings the outward leg of the journey to a close. Directly opposite is a large retail park, with a supermarket and fast food. From here, the best option is to cycle back to Salford by the same route, since it is flat and largely traffic free and is well within most people's capabilities. You can take the train from Moses Gate station, but that is a 7km ride beyond the northern end of the route, and hardly seems worth it. Here are the directions to Moses Gate station: turn left on the far side of the retail park onto the A665 Pilkington Way, then take the A6053 and continue for 5km.

Bury Circular

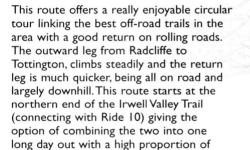

This route offers a really enjoyable circular tour linking the best off-road trails in the area with a good return on rolling roads. The outward leg from Radcliffe to Tottington, climbs steadily and the return leg is much quicker, being all on road and largely downhill. This route starts at the northern end of the Irwell Valley Trail (connecting with Ride 10) giving the option of combining the two into one long day out with a high proportion of good off-road riding.

Manchester, Bolton & Bury Canal

Bury flourished during the industrial revolution and one of the catalysts of expansion was the Manchester, Bolton & Bury Canal. In the late 1700s the MBBC Company was formed to bring coal to the town from Worsley. The canal is no longer navigable, but it does provide the towpath that has recently been successfully transformed into part of the National Cycle Network. The Peel Tower on Holcombe Hill commemorates Sir Robert Peel; a son of Bury, Prime Minister and founder of modern policing.

1 *Start at the northern end of the Irwell Valley Trail (Route 10) in Radcliffe, just north of the River Irwell on Sion Street. Cross the A6053 Pilkington Way into Dale Street. At this point follow the National Cycle Network Route 6 signs, pass a parade of shops and go into Church Street West. Just before the railway bridge over the road turn left and go up the ramp towards Radcliffe Metro station. Cross the station car park and then go over Spring Lane. Join a tarmac path to the left of Coney Green school and follow this to join the towpath of the disused Manchester Bolton & Bury Canal.*

RIDE INFORMATION

Distance	27km (17 miles)
Car-free	5.6km (3.5 miles) (21%)
Grade	Medium

Bike
The off-road trails are well surfaced so any bike should be OK

Suitability for children and beginners?
Sections 1-4 are good, but the complete tour may be too much

Traffic and surface
Traffic is mostly light and the off-road sections are in good condition

Start/finish
Radcliffe, connecting with the Irwell Valley Trail (Ride 10)

Stations
Nearest is Moses Gate, 5.5km west of the start, on the A665 and A6053

Refreshments
Numerous opportunities in the towns and villages en route

What to see
Canals, good off-road trails, viaducts

The Manchester Bolton and Bury Canal.

2 Turn right onto the towpath and head north. The canal is currently disused, but the towpath is in excellent condition, being part of the National Cycle Network. Follow the canal for 1.5km, taking care when passing under bridges as the towpath is narrow and there could be people coming the other way. Leave the canal at a gate on the right to join Hinds Lane and cross the bridge over the canal. Follow Hinds Lane as it climbs past Elton Reservoir. Just after the track enters woods turn left to join another off-road path, this time on a disused railway line.

Canal disused but towpath excellent.

3 The Daisyfield Greenway is also part of NCN Route 6; on joining it, turn right. The Greenway is another well-surfaced trail, giving an excellent route into Bury, particularly as it crosses Wellington Street Viaduct giving good views all around. The viaduct crosses the canal and the path descends to pass between two schools. Follow the NCN signs left towards the town centre.

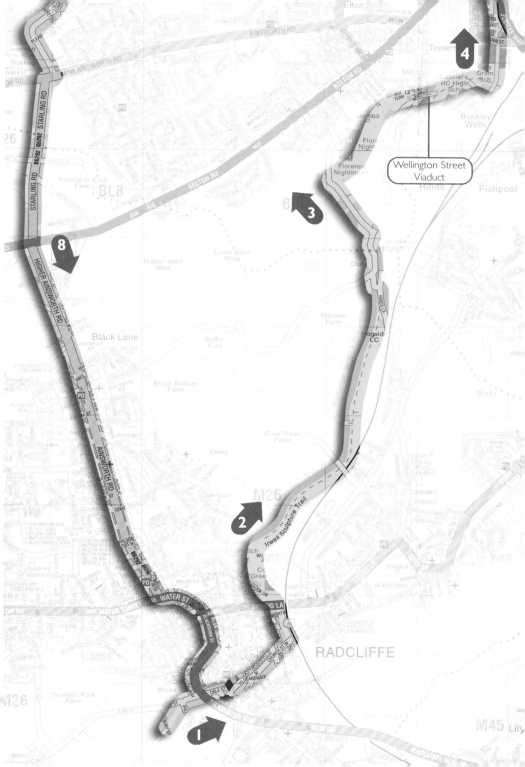

Wellington Street
Viaduct

RIDE
11

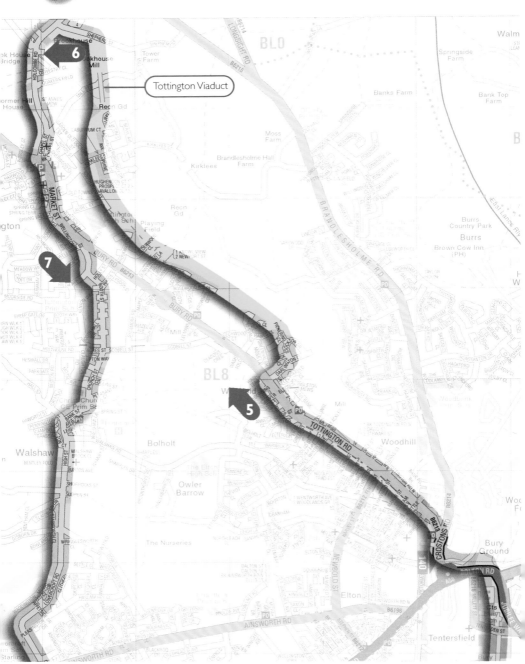

Tottington Viaduct

4 Cross Tenterden Street and go past one of the Sustrans route mile-posts, go under the underpass below Bolton Road, following the signs for Tottington. Go across Crostons Road and turn left to begin to climb Tottington Road, the B6213. The climbing is steep at first then eases. Pass a pub called Pleasant View on the left and continue 1km passing a garage on the left and pub called Wagon Makers on the right; 100m after the pub comes Darlington Close on the right.

5 Turn right into Darlington Close, first left into Stockton Drive and left again into Pickering Close. From the top of Pickering Close go down a short path to join another good stretch of car-free trail. The Kirklees Trail follows another disused railway line, the Holcombe Brook Line, for 2.5km. Another very pleasant trail, the best bit is at the northern end, where Tottington Viaduct carries the path high above woods and lake below. From here it is possible to see the Peel Tower straight ahead on Holcombe Hill.

6 At the top of Shepherd Street turn left into Holcombe Road and head downhill towards Tottington village. Go left, pass the green on the left, then after 500m bear right at the mini roundabout into Booth Street.

7 Over the next few kilometres the road rolls over a couple of short hills. From Tottington you reach Walshaw, another small Pennine village. Turn left into High Street and continue along Lowercroft Road. At the junction with the B6196 go across to Starling Road and begin the long descent back to Radcliffe.

8 Cross over the A58 at the next crossroads and head down a broad, straight road to return to Radcliffe. At the A665 main road, Water Street/Blackburn Street, turn left to the start of the route.

Above: The Kirklees Trail. Below: Sustrans milepost in Bury.

Hollingworth Lake to Watergrove Reservoir

The area known as the South Pennines straddles the Lancashire/Yorkshire divide and has its own character, with small market towns in valleys, canals, features from the cotton industry, high moorland, and reservoirs. From the day-trip resort of Hollingworth Lake to Watergrove Reservoir high on the moors, this mountain bike off-road ride covers all these features in one compact outing, a perfect day's introduction to the diversity of the South Pennines.

The 118-acre Hollingworth Lake and surrounding 'country park' include a nature

RIDE INFORMATION

Distance 22km (14 miles)
Car-free 5.6km (3.5 miles) (25%)
Grade Difficult: a long climb from the valley to the reservoir and rocky trails on the way
Bike Mountain bike

Suitability for children and beginners?

One of the tougher rides in the book, and not for younger children, but take your time and it is quite achievable. However, the excellent path around Watergrove Reservoir up on the moors does make an interesting ride for families with young children

Traffic and surface

Mixture of road and tracks, light traffic on roads

Start/finish

Hollingworth Lake visitor centre has good facilities with an information point, cafe, toilets and parking. Stock up on information as well as food and drink (but don't get too distracted, as there is an excellent ride to be done).

The car park at the Watergrove Reservoir can also be the start/finish of a shorter route around the water, or you can join the Pennine Bridleway (see page 10 for info on the bridleway).

Stations

Littleborough and Smithy Bridge are both close to the starting point

Refreshments

There is a wide choice of pubs and cafes around Hollingworth Lake. The visitor centre has a cafe. Several more pubs lie en route.

What to see

The lake and Watergrove Reservoir (information centre and toilets on far side), Pennine moorland, and great views of Manchester from the high points of the route.

reserve, walking trails, fishing and water sports centre. The lake is actually a feeder reservoir for the Rochdale Canal. In Victorian days there were dance halls here, steamers and even an ice-skating rink for entertaining the local mill workers. The lake was also used by Captain Webb when he was training for the first cross-Channel swim. The place has the air of a seaside resort and remains a thriving centre for water activities.

Set high in the hills above Littleborough and Rochdale the old weaving hamlet of Wardle was once an important staging post on the Long Causeway, the packhorse route over the moors that pre-dates the more modern routes in the valley below.

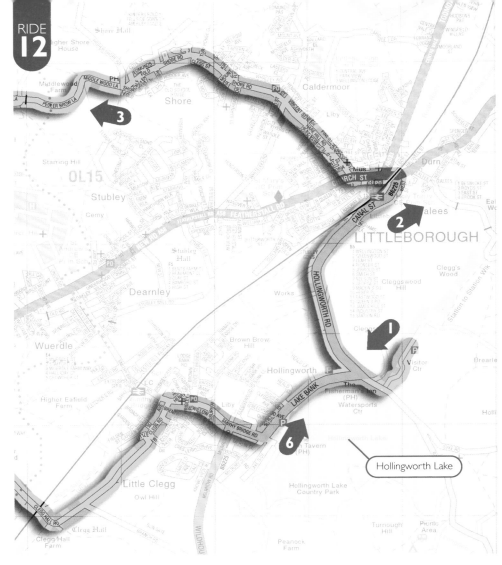

Hollingworth Lake

Watergrove Reservoir was built in the 1930s to improve the water supply to Rochdale and create employment. By 1935, the scheme was providing much-needed work for 550 men. The work took eight years to complete and involved flooding the valley and submerging the village of Watergrove. More recently developed as a nature reserve, the reservoir continues to be Rochdale's main water supply. The excellent path around the reservoir makes an interesting ride for families with young children.

1 *Leave the visitor centre car park and turn right, go past the Fisherman's Inn on the right, and take Hollingworth Road/Canal Street down to Littleborough.*

2 *Turn left to go under the rail bridge and take the A58 Church Street, past the entrance to Littleborough station on the left. Go over a mini-roundabout, then turn right into Hare Hill Road to begin the steady, long climb up to Shore. Follow Shore Road up to its end, where the King William IV pub is on the right.*

Above: The track between Shore and Wardle.
Below left: The Pennine Bridleway passes
through here. Below right: Friendly geese on
the Rochdale Canal.

3 Keeping the pub on the right, carry on up Middlewood Lane, where the route becomes steeper, the tarmac ends and the path becomes rougher. From now on there are good views towards the moors we are heading for. Go through a gate on Pedler Brow Lane and continue straight on (don't go left/downhill on Birch Hill Lane). Follow the track towards the moors, then turn left to drop down into Wardle. In Wardle, come to the village centre, with a large church opposite. Turn right and go uphill

and take the cobbled road up to Watergrove Reservoir. Join the track that goes around the reservoir, riding anticlockwise. Continue on the waymarked trail which climbs above the reservoir. From the highest point on the ride the views back across Manchester are spectacular, and if you look carefully you can see Hollingworth Lake far below.

Once you are back at the reservoir car park begin the descent to the valley bottom – a lot quicker than coming up!

4 Descend through Wardle on Ramsden Road, and fork right onto Wardle Road, which quickly drops to the main A58 Halifax Road.

5 Cross Halifax Road to the left of the roundabout and continue to join Dye House Lane. Follow this over the River Roch. A trainline and Rochdale Canal are all

Views of Hollingworth Lake.

squeezed together in the valley bottom. After the canal continue (on Clegg Hall Road) back to Smithy Bridge (passing close to the station), there turning right back to Hollingworth Lake.

6 Having finished the route take time to enjoy the many refreshment options on the lake front.

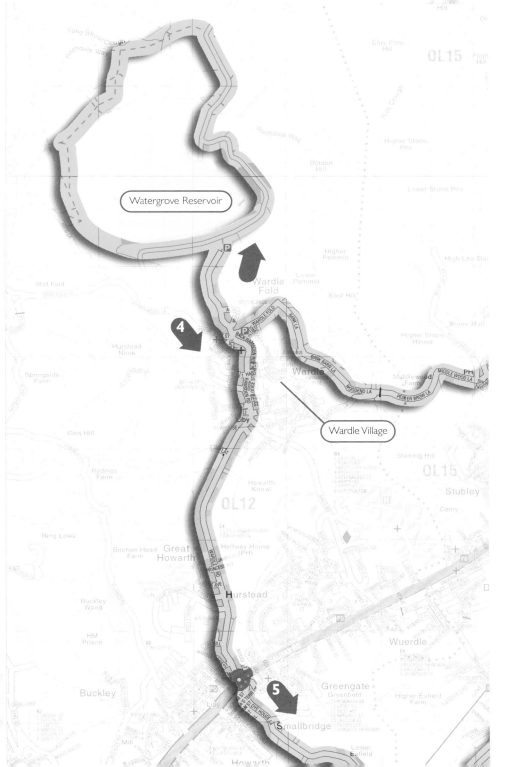

Watergrove Reservoir

Wardle Village

Middlewood Way and Lyme Park

A varied route for riding on a sturdy bike, starting and finishing on a converted railway line and taking in one of Cheshire's finest old houses. There are also fantastic views across Greater Manchester and towards the Peak District.

We start and finish in Marple, to the east of Stockport on the western edge of the Peak District. The town lies at the northern end of the stretch of disused railway line which has been transformed into the Middlewood Way. The trees planted around the trail are maturing and only the straight line of the route gives a clue to its history.

The Middlewood Way

The Macclesfield, Bollington and Marple railway line opened for passenger traffic on 2 August 1869 and closed finally 101 years later, in January 1970. The line was constructed to stimulate trade and industrial development, and for many years carried coal, cotton and passengers back and forth. The line was resurrected as the Middlewood Way 15 years after closure and has become an excellent cycle/walking/horse-riding trail, linking Marple and Macclesfield along the eastern edge of the Cheshire plain. The Middlewood Way has a maturity not yet found in newer trails, and

RIDE INFORMATION

Distance	26km (16 miles)
Car-free	9.6km (6 miles) (37%)
Grade	Medium
Bike	Mountain bike or sturdy-wheeled hybrid recommended

Suitability for children and beginners?

Could be a bit hilly for younger children and complete beginners, but there is the option to stay on the Middlewood Way and miss the climb to Lyme Park

Traffic and surface

Mostly traffic-free, with a few quiet lanes and a short, 3km stretch of busier road from Disley

Start/finish

Rose Hill station on the A626 Stockport Road (small car park in the lane beside the station)

Stations

Rose Hill and Marple

Refreshments

Cafe and Boar's Head pub at old Poynton station, cafe at Lyme Park (open daily in the summer and winter weekends, NT), various services at Disley

What to see

Cheshire countryside, old Poynton station (back across the bridge is the Nelson Pit visitor centre, a useful stop for local information and toilets)

Lyme Park and Hall (National Trust), the Cage (medieval hunting tower, open second and fourth weekends of the month April-October), and superb views

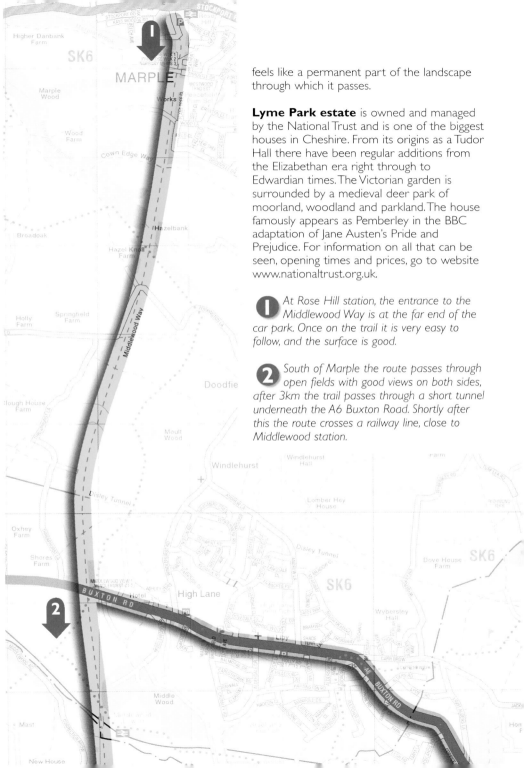

feels like a permanent part of the landscape through which it passes.

Lyme Park estate is owned and managed by the National Trust and is one of the biggest houses in Cheshire. From its origins as a Tudor Hall there have been regular additions from the Elizabethan era right through to Edwardian times. The Victorian garden is surrounded by a medieval deer park of moorland, woodland and parkland. The house famously appears as Pemberley in the BBC adaptation of Jane Austen's Pride and Prejudice. For information on all that can be seen, opening times and prices, go to website www.nationaltrust.org.uk.

❶ *At Rose Hill station, the entrance to the Middlewood Way is at the far end of the car park. Once on the trail it is very easy to follow, and the surface is good.*

❷ *South of Marple the route passes through open fields with good views on both sides, after 3km the trail passes through a short tunnel underneath the A6 Buxton Road. Shortly after this the route crosses a railway line, close to Middlewood station.*

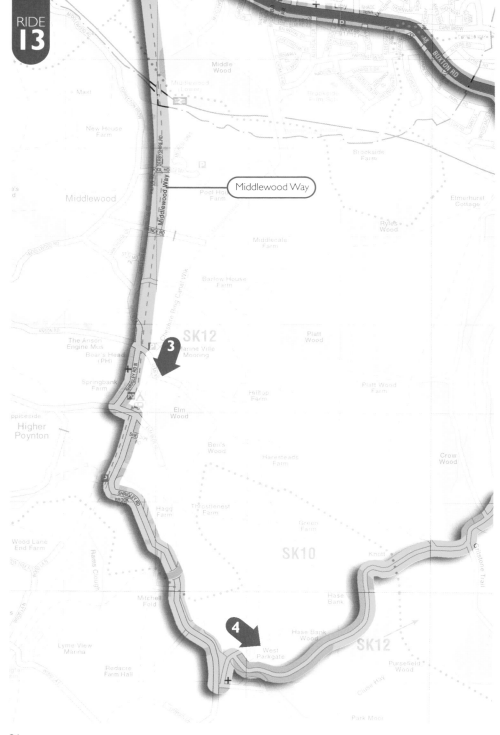

RIDE **13**

Middlewood Way

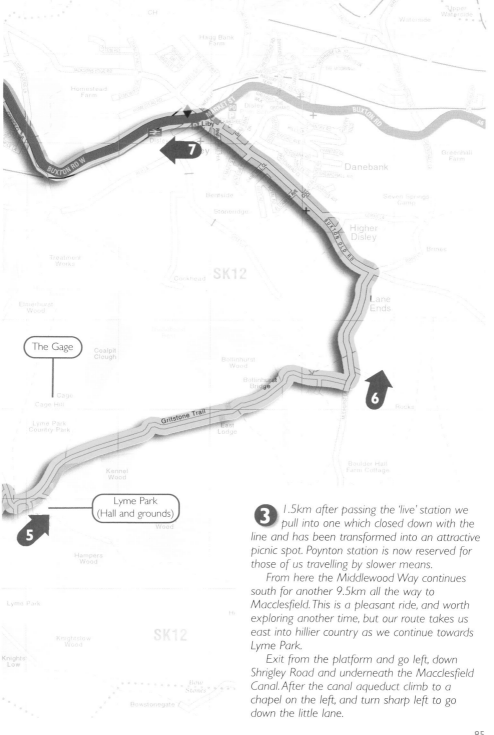

3 1.5km after passing the 'live' station we pull into one which closed down with the line and has been transformed into an attractive picnic spot. Poynton station is now reserved for those of us travelling by slower means.

From here the Middlewood Way continues south for another 9.5km all the way to Macclesfield. This is a pleasant ride, and worth exploring another time, but our route takes us east into hillier country as we continue towards Lyme Park.

Exit from the platform and go left, down Shrigley Road and underneath the Macclesfield Canal. After the canal aqueduct climb to a chapel on the left, and turn sharp left to go down the little lane.

The Gage in Lyme Park.

4 The lane drops to a small gatehouse that marks the western entrance to Lyme Park. It feels like entering the great estate through the back door. Go through the gate to join a pretty woodland track, popular with walkers, which steadily climbs towards Lyme Hall. After 1km leave the woods and come out at a small car park. Take the road from here straight down to Lyme Hall.

5 The route passes the front of the hall and goes towards the East Gate House. Head for the Peak District hills (the Cage is off to the left). Go through the east gate and exit the park. A rough track descends then climbs to join the road.

6 Turn left on to Mudhurst Lane for a long descent into Disley with good views all round. Turn left onto Buxton Old Road and continue to descend. Watch for the traffic humps as you enter Disley – it is possible to pick up a lot of speed down here.

7 In Disley, turn left onto the A6 Buxton Road. Pass Disley station on the left. From here the 3.5km on the A6 may be busy but that is the best return route to the Middlewood Way, and it doesn't take long. Rejoin Middlewood Way 500m after crossing the Macclesfield Canal, where the A6 bridges it. Leave the road on the left, pass under the bridge and rejoin the trail to return to the starting point at Rose Hill station. The return journey from Lyme Park to the finish is very quick, being almost all downhill or flat.

Middlewood Way, south of Marple.

Wilmslow to Tatton Park

This road route is the longest in the book at 32km (20 miles), but being on the Cheshire Plain there are no hills. The complete route makes a full day out, taking some nice quiet 'Cheshire lanes' which make famously good cycling country, and the circuit of historic Tatton Park.

The route is also very flexible – think of it as three rides in one. By using the stations you can start at Wilmslow, ride via Tatton and finish at Knutsford (20km, 12.5 miles). You can also start in Knutsford and simply do the circuit of Tatton Park estate (15km, 9 miles, riding anticlockwise for safer left-turns at all the junctions). For the really ambitious, another option is to connect to Ride 15, Dunham Park to Tatton Park, for a good long ride that continues all the way from Wilmslow to Dunham and back.

Knutsford, it is claimed, gets its name from the Danish King Canute, who apparently forded a river near here in 1016. The town is mentioned in the Domesday Book. Today, Knutsford, together with Wilmslow and Alderley Edge, is one of the most prosperous Cheshire towns. They are all attractive places to explore, and the lanes between them make cycling a real pleasure.

RIDE INFORMATION

Distance 32km (20 miles)
Car-free None

Grade
Medium: the riding is never difficult, but it is a long ride

Bike
Any, but a road bike is recommended

Suitability for children and beginners?
The shorter options are OK

Traffic and surface
Only light traffic apart from the two town centres

Start/finish
Wilmslow, with an option to finish at Knutsford station

Stations
Both Wilmslow and Knutsford, also Mobberley and Ashley en route have stations

Refreshments
Wilmslow and Knutsford centres, Tatton Hall falls halfway round the full route, and makes an ideal stopping point if you plan to ride all the way back to Wilmslow

What to see
Cheshire countryside, Tatton Park (for details see Ride 15)

Above: Mobberley on the Cheshire Cycleway.
Below: Native sheep in Tatton Park.

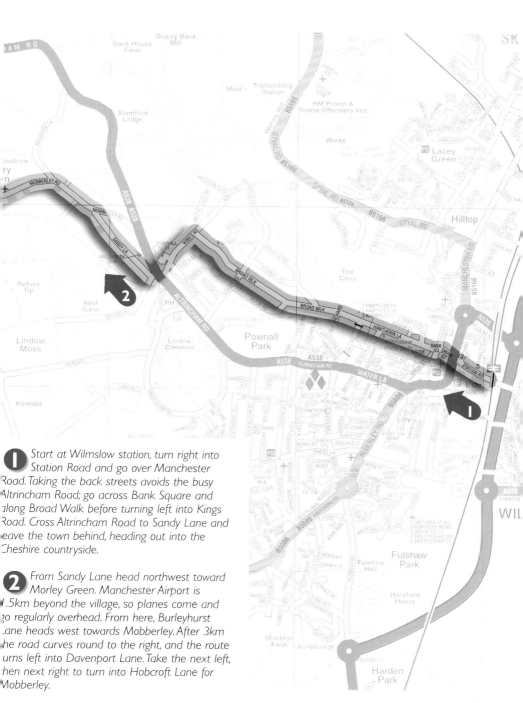

1 Start at Wilmslow station, turn right into Station Road and go over Manchester Road. Taking the back streets avoids the busy Altrincham Road; go across Bank Square and along Broad Walk before turning left into Kings Road. Cross Altrincham Road to Sandy Lane and leave the town behind, heading out into the Cheshire countryside.

2 From Sandy Lane head northwest toward Morley Green. Manchester Airport is 1.5km beyond the village, so planes come and go regularly overhead. From here, Burleyhurst Lane heads west towards Mobberley. After 3km the road curves round to the right, and the route turns left into Davenport Lane. Take the next left, then next right to turn into Hobcroft Lane for Mobberley.

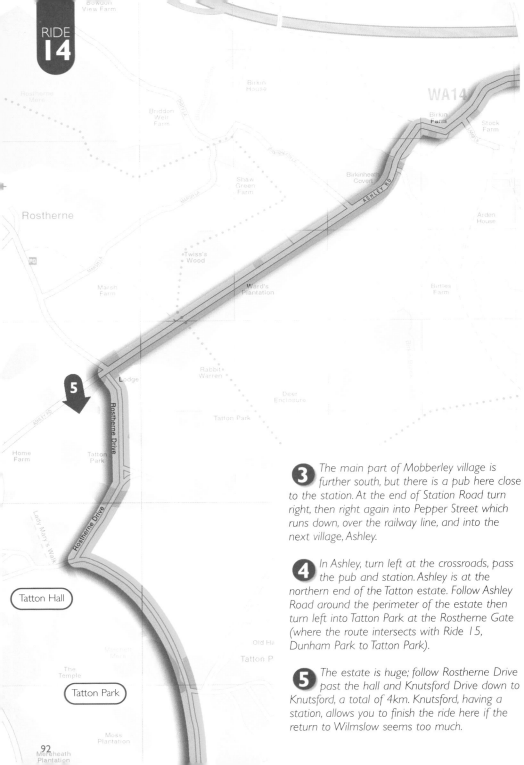

3 The main part of Mobberley village is further south, but there is a pub here close to the station. At the end of Station Road turn right, then right again into Pepper Street which runs down, over the railway line, and into the next village, Ashley.

4 In Ashley, turn left at the crossroads, pass the pub and station. Ashley is at the northern end of the Tatton estate. Follow Ashley Road around the perimeter of the estate then turn left into Tatton Park at the Rostherne Gate (where the route intersects with Ride 15, Dunham Park to Tatton Park).

5 The estate is huge; follow Rostherne Drive past the hall and Knutsford Drive down to Knutsford, a total of 4km. Knutsford, having a station, allows you to finish the ride here if the return to Wilmslow seems too much.

Tatton Hall and Gardens.

6 Continuing from Knutsford, at the end of Knutsford Drive, go right on King Street and pass under the railway. Turn left, and straight away left again into Hollow Lane and left into Mobberley Road to begin the eastward journey back to Wilmslow.

For the third route option (Tatton estate circuit) join the route at Hollow Lane and follow points 7, 3, 4, and 5.

7 After 3km, turn left at Mobberley into Smith Lane, to avoid the busier main road between the two towns. After 1km, turn right into Slade Lane and at the far end turn right onto Hobcroft Lane to begin the return journey in reverse of the outward leg.

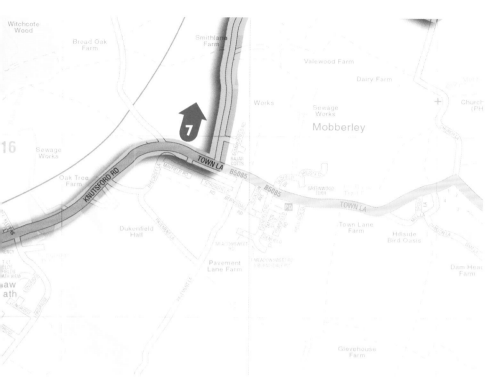

Dunham Park to Tatton Park

Dunham Park, on the southwestern edge of Greater Manchester, makes an ideal starting point for exploring the lanes and villages of Cheshire. The route links two fine country house estates, both of which are managed by the National Trust and are open to the public. Between them lies 11km of quiet lanes and well-tended farmland. Using Knutsford station makes a short one-way ride an option.

This ride connects at the entrance to Tatton Park with Ride 14, Wilmslow to Tatton Park, for more fine Cheshire lane riding.

Tatton Park is a large historic estate run by the National Trust and Cheshire County Council. Roads within the park are open for exploration, and there are many attractions including the two large houses, a working farm, gardens, gift shops and a cafe.

The main hall is early 19th century and is surrounded by Victorian gardens and parkland. The Tudor Old Hall was built around 1520 and has rooms fitted out to demonstrate the changing way of life from then to the mid-20th century. The newer mansion includes state rooms and servants quarters that can be visited. Opening times vary with the seasons, so check in advance (tel 01625 534400, info-line 01625 534435, or website www.tattonpark.org.uk).

RIDE INFORMATION

Distance   22km (14 miles)
Car-free   None
Grade   Medium

Bike   Any bike is suitable

Suitability for children and beginners?
Good for all but younger children

Traffic and surface
Traffic light and surface good

Start/finish
Dunham Park car park, operated by National Trust

Stations
Hale is 3.5km from the start; Knutsford is 2.5km from the southernmost end of the ride

Refreshments
Dunham Park, Tatton Park and several pubs in between

What to see
Dunham Park (see Route 9); Tatton Park (see box), and Rostherne Mere National Nature Reserve, important for water fowl and famous for roosting gulls, with up to 20,000 gathering in winter. There is no access to the lake itself, as it is 'reserved' for the birds, but the view is good from the roadside just past the church outside Rostherne. The Wesley plaque (at point 3, beneath the motorway bridge has two seats), the plaque explaining that from May 1747 onwards John Wesley (the founder of Methodism) on several occasions visited this locality to stay at Old Booth Farm, Agden, preaching under the oak tree which stood in front of the house.

1 Leave Dunham Park by the main gates and turn left, and after just 50m turn left again into Brick Kiln Lane. The lane goes down towards the River Bollin and Dunham Massey Hall can be seen across the fields the left. At the end of the lane is Bollington Mill, and at the rear of the mill take the small footbridge that crosses the river. Across the Bollin is the hamlet of Little Bollington.

2 Little Bollington has a pub with the unusual name, The Swan with Two Nicks, which is on the right just after the river. After this bear left into Park Lane which rises steadily to the A56 Lymm Road. Turn left onto the A56, then with care, go right after 100m into Reddy Lane, signed 1 mile to Millington. From here the route follows typical quiet Cheshire country lanes, with well-kept hedges and fields all around.

3 Reddy Lane passes beneath the M56 (the Wesley plaque is beneath the motorway bridge, left). At Booth Bank take the right fork into Boothbank Lane, go past the first left, under a line of pylons and take the next left, Moss Lane, then left again into Peacock Lane towards Bucklow Hill, passing under the pylons again on the way. At Bucklow Hill go straight over the A556 at the traffic lights, then immediately left into Cicely Mill Lane (not straight on to Tatton Park as signposted).

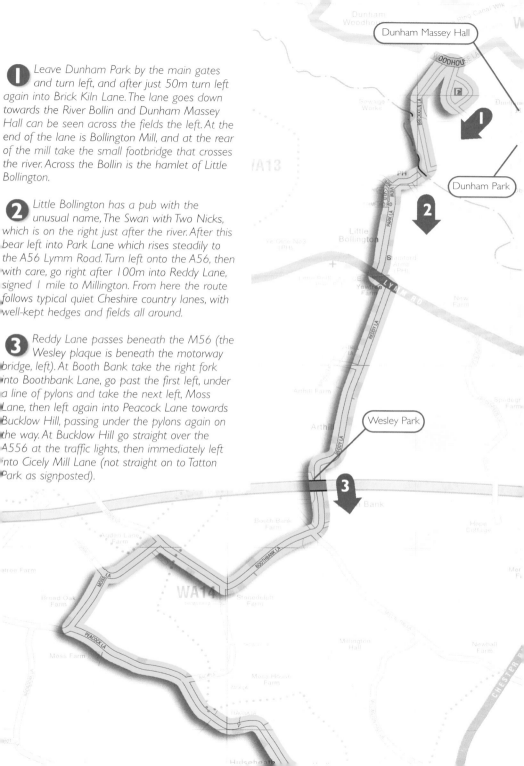

4 Pass a small lake on the right, then you come to a T-junction in the village of Rostherne. Go left for a worthwhile small detour to see Rostherne Mere. To continue, go right for just under 1km to another T-junction, opposite the entrance to Tatton Park.

5 (There is a link here to Ride 14, Wilmslow to Tatton Park.) Cross into the park and follow Rostherne Drive to Tatton Hall.

6 One option is to continue south all the way to Knutsford (2.5km) where you can catch a train. Alternatively, retrace the route to Dunham. Please note: on the return it may look easier and more direct to go straight on at Rostherne and cross the Chester Road by Newhall Farm, but it is actually very difficult to cross the busy road here with traffic moving very quickly.

Rostherne Mere

Tatton Hall

Old Hall

Altrincham to Lymm

Altrincham is a busy town in the borough of Trafford, southwest of Greater Manchester. Less than 2km from the station you can be out in attractive countryside. This route has a figure-of-eight form, heading west to Lymm off-road on the Trans Pennine Trail and returning on-road by quiet lanes.

This route crosses the Bridgewater Canal several times. Built for the Duke of Bridgewater to transport coal from the pits in Worsley it opened in the 1770s. Now, it is popular with anglers, walkers and for narrowboat cruising.

The Trans Pennine Trail (TPT) follows the route of the old railway line between Broadheath and Warrington. The last passenger trains ran in 1962 before falling victim to Dr Beeching's cutbacks. Freight traffic survived until 1985 when the line was closed completely. It has since been converted into a fine trail for walkers, cyclists and horse riders.

One famous landmark in Lymm is the Cross, which stands in the centre of the village. Carved from natural red stone and worn with age, the landmark's origins and history are a mystery, although it is undoubtedly an ancient feature.

1 *Leave the station at Altrincham and turn right into Stamford New Road, then go left then right into Church Street before turning left into Oldfield Road just after the Wheatsheaf pub. After 1km on Oldfield Road, fork right into Seamon's Road. After crossing the Bridgewater Canal take the next path on the left, opposite Atlantic Street, which is the entrance to one of the best uninterrupted stretches of the Trans Pennine Trail.*

RIDE INFORMATION

Distance	21km (13 miles)
Car-free	6.5km (4 miles) (30%)
Grade	Easy/medium
Bike	Any sturdy bike is suitable

Suitability for children and beginners?
Good; younger children could return on the Trans Pennine Trail, reducing the amount of on-road cycling

Traffic and surface
Traffic light, except for the centre of Altrincham. Surface good, the Trans Pennine Trail is firm and generally well drained.

Start/finish
Altrincham town centre

Station
Altrincham

Refreshments
Altrincham, Lymm, and Dunham Woodhouses, which you pass on the outward and return legs

What to see
Bridgewater Canal, excellent off-road trail, and the village of Lymm

Dunham Town Post Office.

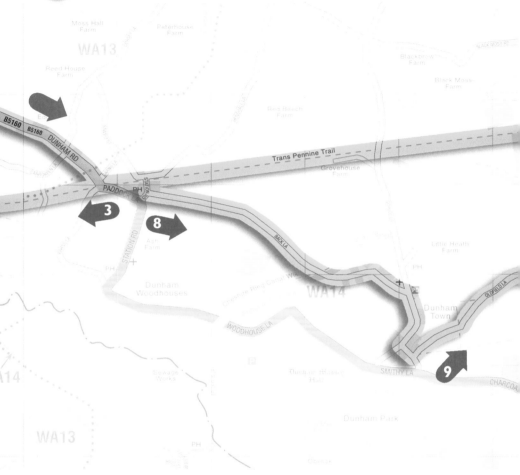

2 Turn left onto the trail; from here there is a 6.5km stretch of well-surfaced, flat and dead straight rail trail. It is very popular, so follow the code of practice for getting along with other users.

3 After just over 2km on the trail pass Dunham Woodhouses (a small diversion left onto Station Road leads to a large pub, the Rope and Anchor, passed again on the return journey). Continue on the trail across the Bollin Valley, crossing the River Bollin shortly before reaching Heatley.

4 At Heatley the trail crosses the A614 and continues directly opposite. (There is a conveniently located bike shop here; Bikes of Lymm.) Continue along the trail for just over 1km before turning left into Reddish Lane, then turn right to cross the Bridgewater Canal into the centre of the attractive Cheshire village of Lymm, where there are plenty of opportunities for eating and drinking.

5 To begin the return journey from Lymm, head back up New Road, re-crossing the canal. Continue on the road instead of rejoining

Below: The route passes over the Bridgewater Canal.

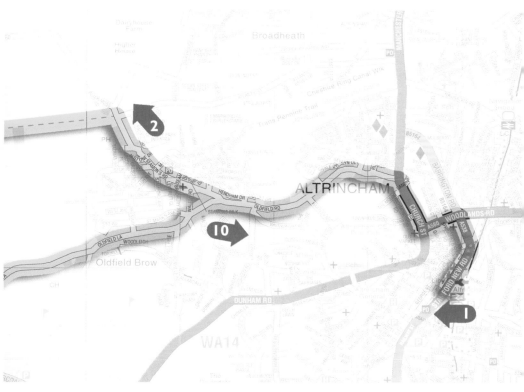

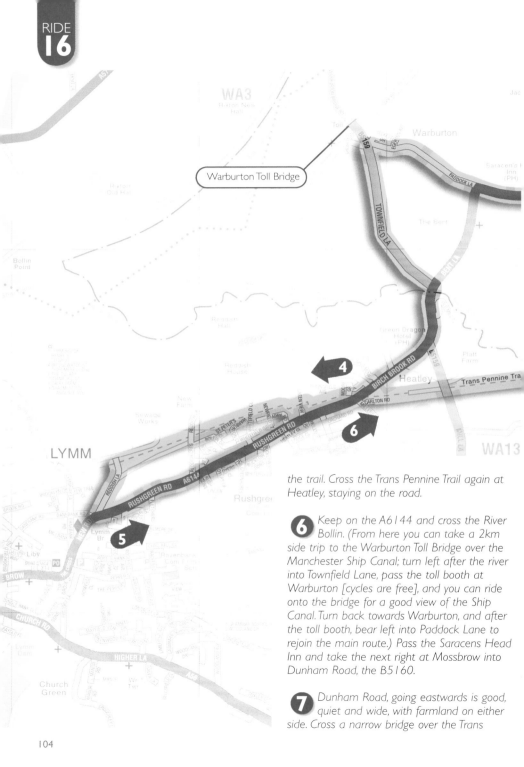

Warburton Toll Bridge

WA3

WA13

LYMM

the trail. Cross the Trans Pennine Trail again at Heatley, staying on the road.

6 Keep on the A6144 and cross the River Bollin. (From here you can take a 2km side trip to the Warburton Toll Bridge over the Manchester Ship Canal; turn left after the river into Townfield Lane, pass the toll booth at Warburton [cycles are free], and you can ride onto the bridge for a good view of the Ship Canal. Turn back towards Warburton, and after the toll booth, bear left into Paddock Lane to rejoin the main route.) Pass the Saracens Head Inn and take the next right at Mossbrow into Dunham Road, the B5160.

7 Dunham Road, going eastwards is good, quiet and wide, with farmland on either side. Cross a narrow bridge over the Trans

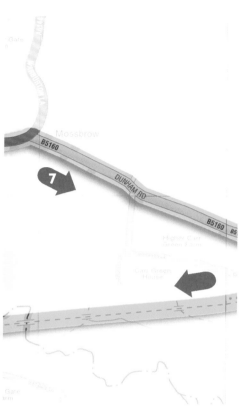

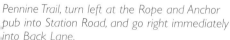

Pennine Trail, turn left at the Rope and Anchor pub into Station Road, and go right immediately into Back Lane.

8 Back Lane winds through fields, and over the Bridgewater Canal on another tight bridge – beware of oncoming traffic. In Dunham Town turn right into School Lane, then left and left again into Oldfield Lane.

9 Oldfield Lane is very narrow in places so be wary of oncoming cars. There are good views to the north across the valley from the lane. At the junction with Seamon's Road turn right.

10 Retrace the outward route along Oldfield Lane and Church Street back to the centre of Altrincham.

The Ride to Wigan Pier

Wigan Pier will always be linked with George Orwell's account of the lives and hardships of 1930s mill workers and miners, and has progressed to become a modern visitor attraction that looks back to those hard times. Taking the pier and mills as a starting point this any-bike ride follows the Leeds & Liverpool Canal to escape to Haigh Country Park.

The Leeds & Liverpool Canal was completed in 1816, and at 203km (127 miles) is the longest canal in Britain. At Leeds it links to the Aire & Calder Navigation to create a continuous waterlink between the Irish Sea and the North Sea. The canal was built to carry coal and cotton but fell into disuse as the railways developed. Recently, much work has been done to restore the canal for navigation and improve the towpaths. They make excellent routes for cycling.

Wigan Pier is a great day out for all. The complex houses a fantastic range of attractions: see life in Wigan in 1900 in the museum The Way We Were, ride a waterbus on the canal,

RIDE INFORMATION

Distance	25 km (16 miles)
Car-free	12.5km (8 miles) (50%)
Grade	Medium: a long ride, but no major difficulties

Bike
Any bike with sturdy wheels will cope; there's just one short rough stretch

Suitability for children and beginners?
Good, although it is one of the longer rides

Traffic and surface
Half is traffic-free track or towpath, the rest mostly minor roads

Start/finish
Wigan Pier, close to the centre of Wigan and both railway stations, plenty of parking

Stations
Wigan North Western and Wigan Wallgate are on different lines, but both are very close to the start

Refreshments
Good cafes at Trencherfield Mill at the start/finish, Haigh Hall (in the country park) and in Standish town.

The route also passes several pubs, the Commercial Inn and Kirklees Hall pubs are both are very close to the top of the lock flight

What to see
The Wigan Pier museum complex is well worth visiting, and includes the world's largest mill steam engine (careful, or you could spend the day here without going on the ride – and that is pretty good too!), the 21-lock flight on the Leeds & Liverpool Canal, and Haigh Country Park attractions

Trenchefield Mill at Wigan Pier.

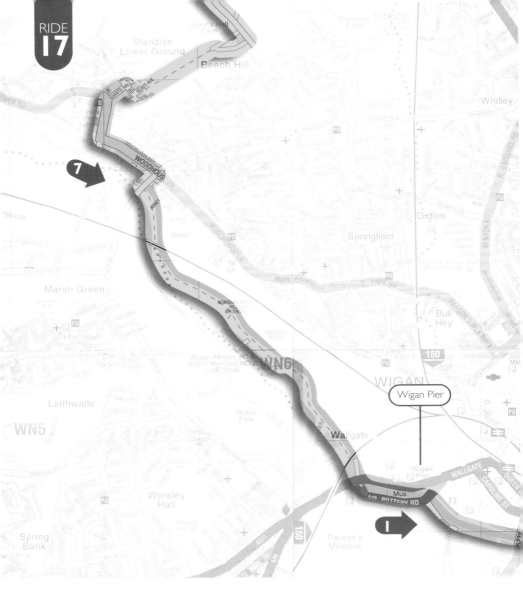

experience the amazing 'World's largest working mill steam engine' and the working cotton looms in Trencherfield Mill. There is also Opie's Museum of Memories, which reflects domestic life in 20th-century Britain.

Haigh Country Park has miles of tracks to explore by bike – just remember pedestrians have right of way. The cafe in the stable block is very good, and there's an information centre, a craft gallery and a miniature railway which gives rides at weekends. Special events such as carnivals and rallies are also held. Call Haigh Country Park (tel 01942 832895) for details.

1 *The start is at Wigan Pier. Join the towpath of the Leeds & Liverpool Canal (going east – with Trencherfield Mill behind you, turn left). The first lock is Bottom Lock, the lowest in a remarkable flight of 21.*

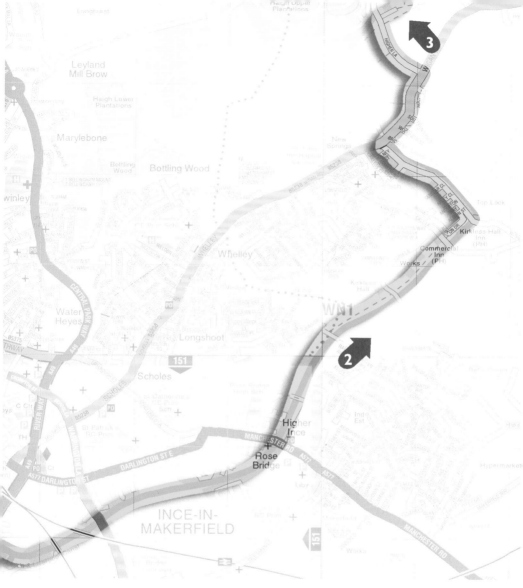

2 *Follow the towpath up the flight on what may be the hilliest towpath ride ever – fortunately the path is in excellent condition. In a couple of places it is necessary to cross roads which the canal passes under. On reaching the Top Lock turn left onto Withington Lane. Follow this to the first road to cross the canal, Wigan Road, and turn right here over the canal and up the hill. Caution here, as the road is narrow and quite busy – it may be a good idea to walk over the bridge on the pavement.*

3 *Turn left into Higher Lane, cross a hump-back bridge then immediately turn right onto the bridleway which climbs to the village of Haigh. At the top of the bridleway go left between the church and the pub (the Balcarres Arms) onto Copperas Lane. This is the highest point on the route. This lane gives a fast descent to Haigh Hall, but do check out the windmill in the field on the left.*

4 At the bottom of Copperas Lane go into Haigh Country Park (cafe and attractions). Leave the park and turn left onto School Lane. Go down the hill to the junction with Red Rock Lane, follow this down over the Leeds & Liverpool Canal and continue to the junction with Chorley Road.

5 Turn right onto the A5106, Chorley Road, and after 400m go left into Rectory Lane, towards Standish. Pass under a railway bridge and continue to Standish.

6 In Standish at traffic lights, head straight over, then after a second set of lights in School Lane, turn left in front of a church. Take Beech Walk, an unsurfaced road which runs into Standish Wood Lane and gradually drops towards

Standish Lower Ground back to the canal. A couple of rougher sections here are not too long and can be walked as the path soon improves. Turn right onto a small path gently downhill and come out in a housing estate, continue on down to Woodhouse Drive.

7 Follow Woodhouse Drive to the first traffic lights, go right over the bridge and turn right immediately onto a path which leads down to the canal. Turn right again onto the towpath towards Wigan and follow it back to Wigan Pier. On the way you pass the JJB stadium, home of Wigan Athletic FC and the Wigan Warriors Rugby League team.

At the top of the rise of locks from Wigan.

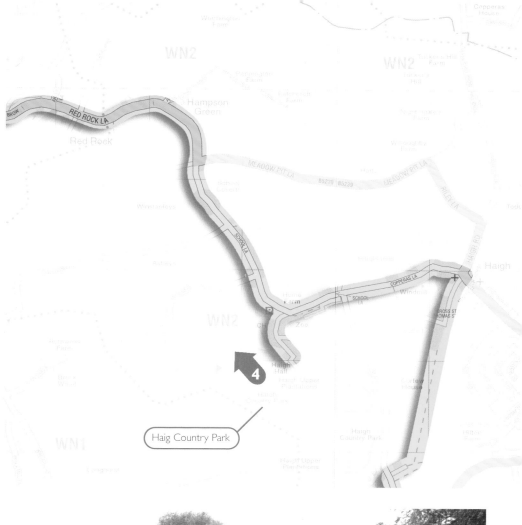

Haig Country Park

Adlington Hilly Road Ride

This any-bike route explores lanes around reservoirs and the West Pennine Moors. From Adlington the route climbs steeply at times onto the moors above Rivington, returning through Lever Park. The area played host to the Commonwealth Games Road Race 2002, but while the hills were a considerable challenge for the racers over many laps, they are quite manageable over our one circuit.

There has been a settlement in Adlington since about 650AD and records exist from the 12th century. During the 19th century the town grew rapidly, with the development of the industries of cotton spinning, dyeing and weaving. Coal mining took place in the area from 1350 all the way until the 1980s, and this supported the industrial development, but has now ceased. Adlington was such a thriving town that, in addition to the canal, it once had three railway stations.

RIDE INFORMATION

Distance   16km (10 miles)
Car-free   None

Grade
Difficult: although not long this is the hilliest route in the book. The hills are a rewarding challenge to complete

Bike
Any bike is suitable, make sure the gears are working - you will need them all

Suitability for children and beginners?
Not recommended

Traffic and surface
Light traffic and mostly quiet lanes

Start/finish
Adlington. Alternatively, if car-based, start at Great House Barn in Rivington Country Park

Stations
Adlington station, on the line between Bolton and Preston

There isn't much parking space at the station so if travelling by car it may be better to start on the other side of the route, at Great House Barn in Rivington Country Park (although that can be very busy at weekends)

Refreshments
Pubs en route, also Adlington, Rivington village, cafe at the Great House Barn in Rivington Country Park

What to see
Reservoirs, moors, and the Great House Barn in Rivington Country Park (the information centre has details of local attractions and landscape)

The stocks on the green at Rivington.

 If travelling by train, start at Adlington station. From there turn right into Railway Road and climb steadily towards the West Pennine hills ahead. Cross at the traffic lights (Elephant and Castle pub on the right) into Babylon Lane, continue climbing and eventually ride out of Adlington into open country. Turn left at the next junction (Long Lane, ignoring the 'cycle route straight on' sign) by the Bay Horse Hotel.

2 Long Lane runs parallel to the M61 for 2km, with good views to the right to the moors, then drops into the village of Limbrick. Make a sharp right turn 100m after the Black Horse pub (which has apparently been serving locals their ale for over 1,000 years!) into Back Lane.

3 Begin climbing again on the lane, steeply at first, passing under the motorway. The road soon levels out with Anglezarke Reservoir on the left. At the next T-junction, with Yew Tree pub opposite, turn left and cross the end of the reservoir. Follow the edge of the reservoir round and then bear right uphill at the next junction, into Parson's Bullough Road.

4 These roads were used in the 2002 Commonwealth Games Road Race and this was one of the main climbs in the race. From Anglezarke Reservoir climb up to Yarrow Reservoir, across the River Yarrow, then up again from Alance Bridge to emerge eventually into open moorland. At the next junction bear right into Sheep House Lane and begin the long fast descent to the village of Rivington. This is a pretty

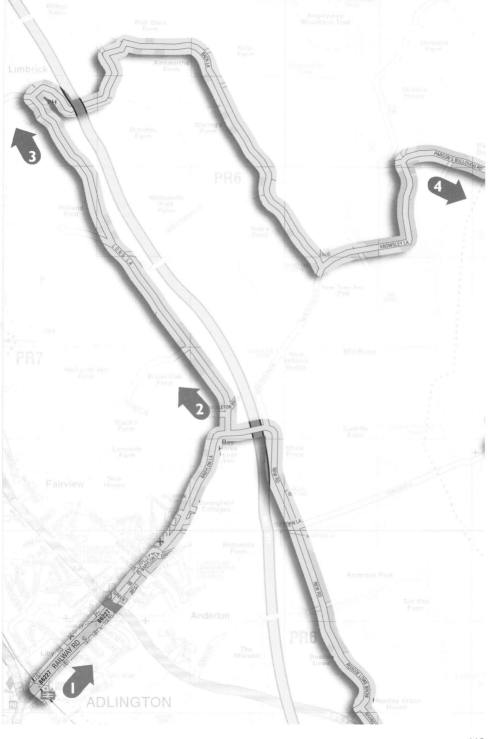

Below: High above Yarrow Reservoir.

little hamlet with a cafe, and stocks on the village green. At the village green turn left with care – this turn caused crashes in the Games, when the roads were damp.

5 Follow Rivington Lane through Lever Park/Rivington Country Park (where the Great House Barn on the right has a cafe and a shop). Continue along Rivington Lane.

6 At the southern end of Lever Park turn right into Dryfield Lane, pass beside the water treatment works (which turns the reservoir water into drinking water), and continue to the junction with the A673. Turn right for a short stretch of busier road, up to Grimeford village. Turn right carefully into Rivington Lane, by the Millstone Hotel.

7 Follow Roscoe Lower Brow/New Road back up towards the M61, and bear left over the motorway. Close the circuit at the Bay Horse pub, and go left to follow Babylon Lane for the final descent through Adlington to the railway station.

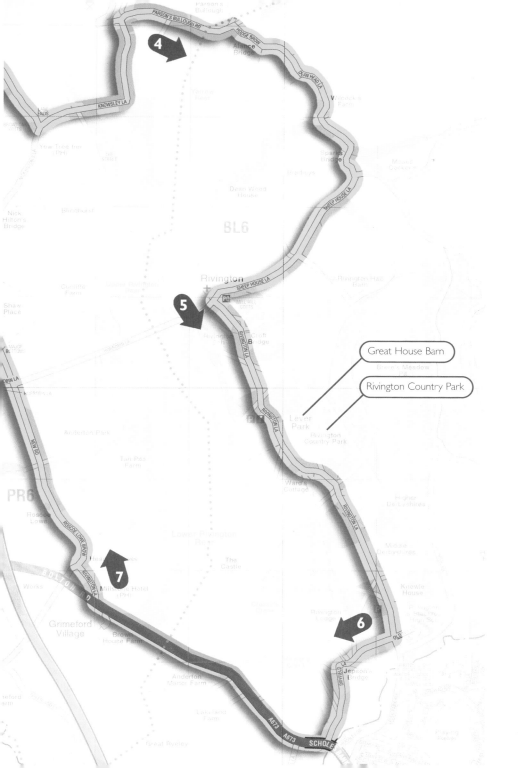

Great House Barn

Rivington Country Park

Lever Park Off-road

Lever Park was the venue for the Mountain bike race in the 2002 Commonwealth Games – but don't worry, this is a much more leisurely exploration of a lovely venue. Highly recommended as a gentle off-road ride, there is lots of interest packed into a short outing in attractive surroundings. As a bonus, you are never far from a cafe!

The riding is good with well-drained paths and tracks. Using the many bridleways around here you could easily form a more ambitious ride, for example, to Rivington Pike high on the moors above the park.

The Rivington Reservoirs were the first to be constructed when, in the late 1840s, the city fathers of Liverpool realised they had to create a water supply to feed the growing city. Water was first piped 30km southwest to Liverpool in 1857. The reservoirs hold over

4,000 million gallons of water, yet demand soon outstripped supply and Liverpool had to look to the Lake District and North Wales for more water.

The Rivington and Great House Barns are both thought to be Saxon in origin although much renovated. Massive oak trusses stand on stone bases to support the pitched stone roofs.

The castle. When Lord Leverhulme purchased Lever Park in 1900 he made many changes, including renovating the two barns and constructing terraced gardens. He also built a scale replica of Liverpool Castle, which was demolished in 1725 after being badly damaged during the Civil War 1642-50. Between 1912 and 1925 he worked on this folly to recreate the castle relic. Leverhulme's project was never completed, but since he was building a ruin you'd never know, and now

RIDE INFORMATION

Distance 7km (4 miles)
Car-free 6.6km (4 miles) (95%)
Grade Easy

Bike Mountain bike

Suitability for children and beginners?
Good

Traffic and surface
Entirely off-road (bar two very short stretches)

Start/finish
Great House Barn information centre (cafe

and shop, information centre next door, and car park)

Stations
Blackrod and Adlington stations, 4km from start on the Bolton-Preston line

Refreshments
Both Great House and Rivington Hall Barns serve food and drinks

What to see
Lever Park has many attractions, fine woodland paths, the reservoirs, the ancient barns and the mock castle

Above: Great House Barn in Lever Park.
Below: Fantastic woodland trails.

it looks as if it really could be hundreds of years old.

Rivington is an ancient village with evidence of habitation since Anglo-Saxon times. There has been a church here since 1540, and the 'new' chapel was built in 1703. Many cottages were used for hand weaving, but by the mid-1800s the large mills were taking over. The construction of the reservoirs led to the lower part of the village being flooded but Rivington has changed little since then.

1 *Set off from the Great House Barn and head down past the car park towards the reservoir. After 100m, turn right to join a track which runs along a broad tree-lined avenue. The track runs into a surfaced road which passes Rivington School.*

2 *Turn right into Sheep House Lane and head uphill towards the ancient village of Rivington. Turn right into Rivington Lane in front of the village green.*

Below: Lower Rivington Reservoir.

3 *Take the first left after the village up the wide bridleway which climbs to Rivington Hall Barn.*

4 *Go through the barn car park, passing to its left, and take the uphill track. Follow this up the left side of the clough, around the top and back down the other side. At the bottom of the clough bear left and take the broad tree-lined track which joins a surfaced road and passes behind Rivington High School.*

5 *Follow the road round to the right beside the school and pass in front, turn right into Rivington Lane before taking the first left into Dryfield Lane. Take the first right off-road again on a bridleway along the rear of sports pitches. On re-entering the woodland, bear left towards the reservoir and the castle.*

6 *From the castle follow the path beside the reservoir, returning to the starting point at Great House Barn.*

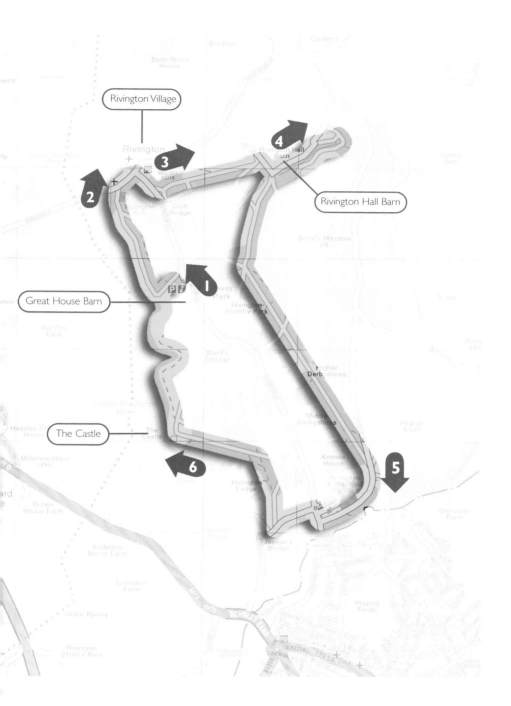

Rivington Village

Rivington Hall Barn

Great House Barn

The Castle

Bromley Cross to reservoirs and West Pennine moors

From the outskirts of Bolton up on to the West Pennine moors this road-bike route is fairly hilly, with views that make the effort worthwhile. The Strawberry Duck at Entwistle makes an ideal halfway pub stop.

Wayoh Reservoir lies between Edgworth, Entwistle and Chapeltown and is one of a chain of reservoirs providing water for the Bolton area. It was originally built in the 19th century then enlarged in the early 1960s. The surrounding area is now a nature reserve. Together with Turton and Entwistle Reservoir, Wayoh provides up to 50 per cent of Bolton's drinking water. Being surrounded by forests of fir trees, they have a very different character to higher, more exposed moorland reservoirs.

The Lancashire Cycleway is a 162km (260-mile) route of northern and southern loops which meet at Whalley in the Ribble Valley. The cycleway follows minor roads and explores all corners of Lancashire. More information from website www.lancashire.gov.uk/environment/cycling/index.asp.

RIDE INFORMATION

Distance 20km (12 miles)
Car-free None
Grade Medium; a couple of stiff climbs

Bike
A road bike is OK, although there is one short section of rougher track at Entwistle

Suitability for children and beginners?
Not for complete beginners or small children, but fine if you don't rush round. You can get on a train at Entwistle which halves the distance.

Remember the weather turns very quickly on the moors. Always take a windproof jacket just in case

Traffic and surface
Traffic is generally light, the short stretches on the A666 Blackburn Road are busiest – be careful crossing

Start/finish
Bromley Cross station on the Bolton-Blackburn line, on the northern outskirts of Bolton, 4km from the centre

Stations
Bromley Cross station and Entwistle station lies halfway round the route

Refreshments
The Strawberry Duck pub (food all day) at Entwistle is the ideal stopping point, and there are pubs in Edgworth and Egerton

What to see
Highlights are the reservoirs of Wayoh and Turton and the moorland views in the second half.

The misty Turton and Entwhistle Reservoir.

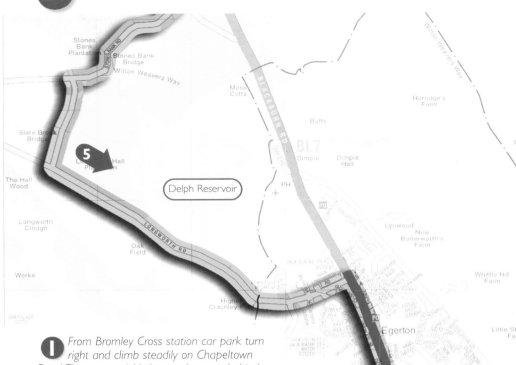

Delph Reservoir

1 *From Bromley Cross station car park turn right and climb steadily on Chapeltown Road. The route quickly leaves the town behind with good views to the right overlooking the valley which holds Jumbles Reservoir and Country Park. Pass under a railway bridge and before entering Chapeltown follow the road round to the right onto Wellington Road, which descends to Turton Bottoms. From Turton Bottoms quickly get in a low gear for the sharp climb up to Edgworth. The climb continues way up on to the moors.*

2 *In Edgworth, turn left at the crossroads (White Horse pub on the left) onto Blackburn Road. After 1km, turn left into Hob Lane – be careful as the lane is steep and narrow with a sharp turn at the bottom. The road crosses Wayoh Reservoir via a causeway. There should be water on both sides, but after a dry summer levels maybe very low. After the reservoir comes a short steep climb before passing Entwistle station. This can provide an early escape should the weather or the lure of the Strawberry Duck prevent you continuing.*

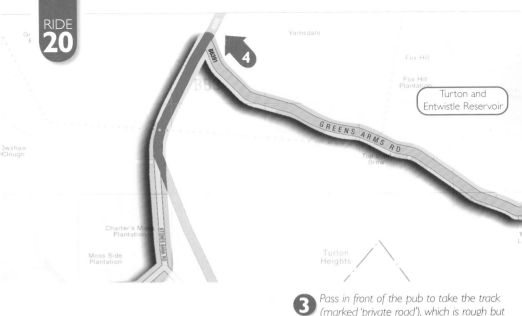

Wayoh Reservoir runs low on water.
Opposite: Turton and Entwhistle Reservoir,
and the moors behind.

3 Pass in front of the pub to take the track (marked 'private road'), which is rough but passable with care on a road bike. This track meets the head of the second reservoir, Turton and Entwistle, which is very attractive surrounded by woodland. There is a small car park and picnic spot at the western end of the dam, just before the road climbs from the valley back up onto the moors. At the next junction, turn right onto Greens Arms Road (B6391) for a nice longer stretch curving gently down to meet the A666 Blackburn Road. At the junction there, turn left onto the Lancashire Cycleway

4 After just under 1km on the A666, carefully take the first possible right turn, staying on the Lancashire Cycleway. Be alert and dismount if you feel safer – it is on a fast bend. Pass through a little forest, then turn right and descend through the woods. Turn left (the Cycleway goes straight on to Belmont), then take the next left onto Longworth Road. Roll gently downhill, with Delph Reservoir on the left, towards Egerton.

5 At Egerton, turn right back onto the A666 (now it is almost all downhill back to the starting point). From the A666 take the next left fork onto Darwen Road (B6472). Continue down and finally turn left just before a railway bridge, back onto Chapeltown Road. This is 200m from the start/finish at Bromley Cross station. If in need of further refreshment there is a pub, The Railway, opposite the station.

ACKNOWLEDGEMENTS

Without the help and support of many people this would have been a much more difficult project to complete. So thanks must go to local authority cycling officers for all their advice and work on behalf of cyclists, to Nicky Crowther for such helpful guidance, to friends at the Cycling Project (keep up the good work), and to my cycling friends who've put up with me rambling on about Manchester for what seems like forever. Let's go riding again, I know some good routes.

Mapping reproduced from Philip's Bristol & Bath Street Atlas © Philip's 2003 Cartography by Philip's This product includes mapping data licensed from Ordnance Survey ® with the permission of the Controller of Her Majesty's Stationary Office. © Crown copyright 2003. All rights reserved. Licence number 100011710.

Author	**Neil Simpson**
Project Manager	**Louise McIntyre**
Editor	**Nicky Crowther**
Design	**Simon Larkin**
Page Layout	**Chris Fayers**
	James Robertson
Photography	**Neil Simpson**
Front cover photo	**Emma Wood**